Progressive
HARMONICA METHOD

by
William Lee Johnson

Visit our Website
www.learntoplaymusic.com

The Progressive Series of Music Instruction Books, CDs, and DVDs

CD TRACK LISTING

1	Lesson 2 Ex 1-3	15	Lesson 16 Taps – My Country 'Tis of Thee
2	Lesson 3 Ex 4-10	16	Lesson 17 – Ode to Joy – Bach's Minuet in G
3	Lesson 4 Ex 11-13	17	Lesson 18 – Silent Night – Jingle Bells
4	Lesson 5 Ex 14	18	Lesson 19 Ex 52-57
5	Lesson 6 Ex 15-16	19	Lesson 20 Ex 58 – Irish Washer Woman
6	Lesson 7 Ex 17-22	20	Lesson 21 Ex 59 – God Rest Ye Merry Gentlemen
7	Lesson 8 Ex 23 – Oh When the Saints Go Marchin' In	21	Lesson 22 Ex 63 – What Shall We Do With The Drunken Sailor
8	Lesson 9 Ex 26 For He's a Jolly Good Fellow	22	Preview – Blues Harmonica Method
9	Lesson 10 Ex 27-36	23	Preview – Rhythm Guitar
10	Lesson 11 Good King Wenceslaus – Amazing Grace	24	Preview – Lead Guitar
11	Lesson 12 – Twelve Bar Chord Structure in the Key of G	25	Preview – Rock Guitar Method
12	Lesson 13 – The Crosstown 12 Bar Blues – The Basic Boogie Woogie	26	Preview – Slide Guitar Techniques
13	Lesson 14 Ex 37-45	27	Preview – Fingerpicking Licks
14	Lesson 15 Ex 46 – No Frills Rolling Rock	28	Preview – Bass Guitar
		29	Preview – Bass Licks

Acknowledgements
Cover Photograph: Phil Martin

For further information contact:
LTP Publications
Email: info@learntoplaymusic.com.au
www.learntoplaymusic.com

I.S.B.N. 0 947183 84 1
Order Codes: CP-18384

COPYRIGHT CONDITIONS
No part of this book can be reproduced in any form without written consent of the publisher.

© 2004 L.T.P. Publishing Pty. Ltd.

Contents

Introduction 5

Section One 6

Lesson 1
Which Harmonica To Use
With This Book 6

Lesson 2
Holding the Harmonica 9

Lesson 3
Playing to the Basic Beat 13

Lesson 4
Harmonica Chords 17

Lesson 5
About Single Notes:
Read, But Don't Worry 21

Lesson 6
About Written Notation
Systems For The Harmonica 24

Lesson 7
Playing Songs And
Rhythms From Notation 26

Lesson 8
About the Major Scale 29
**Twinkle Twinkle
   Little Star-1** 31
**Oh When the Saints Go
   Marching In** 32

Lesson 9
More Simple Songs
With One Note Per Beat 33
**For He's A Jolly
   Good Fellow** 34
On Top of Old Smoky 35

Lesson 10
About The Alternate
Major Scales 37

Lesson 11
More Songs 40
Good King Wenceslaus 40
Red River Valley 41
Amazing Grace 42

Lesson 12
About Improvisation 43

Section Two 45

Lesson 13
The Cross Town
Twelve Bar Blues 46
**The Cross Town Arpeggiated
   Twelve Bar Blues** 47
The Basic Boogie Woogie 48

Lesson 14
More Rhythm:
Breaking Beats Into Parts 49
**Twinkle Twinkle
   Little Star-2** 51

Lesson 15
Rhythm Variations
On The Doublet Pattern 53
**The Two-Timing
   Twelve Bar Blues** 55
The No Frills Rollin' Rock 56

Lesson 16
More Songs That Use
Partial Beats 57
Taps 57
Old Folks at Home 57
My Country 'Tis of Thee 58

Contents (cont.)

Lesson 17
About Classical Music 59
**Ode To Joy
(Beethoven's Ninth)**................ 59
Brahm's Lullaby 60
**Bach's Minuet in G
(C, for You)** 60

Lesson 18
Some Holiday Hits 61
Silent Night 61
Auld Lang Syne 62
Jingle Bells 63

Lesson 19
More Train Time 64
Mister Lee's Freight Train 66

Lesson 20
Triplet Rhythms 67
Row Row Row Your Boat 67
Arkansaw Traveller 68
Irish Washerwoman 69

Lesson 21
Playing The Minor Scale 70
Greensleeves 71
**God Rest Ye Merry
Gentlemen** 72

Lesson 22
Playing The Dorian Scale 73
Saint James Infirmary 74
House of the Rising Sun 74
**What Shall We Do With
A Drunken Sailor** 75

Appendix A
Playing With Others 76

Appendix B
Reading Standard Notation
For The Harmonica 79

Introduction

The harmonica is an easy instrument for beginners to play, as many of the physical techniques used in playing are those that you already practice every day, when breathing and talking. It is a difficult instrument to master, because so many of the more subtle and advanced techniques take place out of sight, inside the mouth. To reflect this "easy/difficult" division, the *Progressive Harmonica Method* is divided into two sections.

Section One will provide you, the beginning harmonica student, with a good technical and theoretical base from which to continue playing. Lessons One through Twelve will allow you to play simple tunes and exercises with an absolute minimum of technique. These early lessons will focus on solo playing skills.

Section Two, including Lessons Thirteen through Twenty Two, will begin to require your ability to obtain single notes, and to maintain a steady rhythm. Folk and classical styles will be emphasized, and a taste of blues and rock will be included, although blues or rock enthusiasts will want to follow their use of this method book with a study of *Progressive Blues Harmonica*, which is entirely devoted to those types of music. A *Supplementary Songbook* is also available to be used while working with this method book (see page 78).

For those with no musical background, whenever a musical term or concept is introduced, it will be explained. Standard musical notation is not used throughout most of this book. The ten hole harmonica is not well adapted to playing from standard notation, and little harmonica music is available in the form of standard notation. However, for those who wish to be able to play from standard notation, an explanation is provided in the Appendix.

It is recommended that beginners practice in short (15-30 minute) sessions, at least once or twice a day. As soon as the material in Section One begins to seem familiar (1-4 hours of practice for the "average" student), it is time to progress to Section Two. Remember: It is important to play both satisfying easy material and to practice unmastered techniques in each daily session.

SECTION ONE
Lesson 1
Which Harmonica To Use With This Book

The small and inexpensive instrument known as the **"Ten Hole"**, the **"Diatonic"**, the **"Major"**, or the **"Blues"** harmonica (or **"harp"**) is the most common and easily available type of harmonica, though many other types do exist. It can be used to play almost any style of music, however it is most often associated with folk, blues, rock and country.

This instructional package is designed primarily for use with a ten hole harmonica of the above type. Make sure that your harmonica has ten holes, is "diatonic-tuned" or "Major-tuned", and is in the "key of C" (explained below) before you purchase it.

There are many available brands and models of harmonicas appropriate for use with this book. Although their prices range from under $10.00 US to over $30.00 US, any of these models are fine for the beginner. But be aware that an instrument costing less than $8.00 US ($10.00 Aust) (£5.00 British) may be of inferior construction, and is likely to be harder to play.

Wood or Plastic? And What Shape?

The portion of the harmonica containing the ten holes is called the "comb" (see The Parts of the Harmonica diagram, following). Beginners may find that harmonicas with plastic combs feel smoother and more comfortable on the lips than those with wooden combs. Shapes of harmonicas vary slightly, from the more square to the more rounded, but do not affect either the sound or the ease of playing.

Most music stores should have a selection of appropriate instruments, so choose one that appeals to you, or falls within your price range. Some of the more common brands are Hohner (e.g. Hohner Marine Band, Hohner Golden Melody), Huang (e.g. Huang Silvertone Deluxe, Huang Star Performer), and Tombo (Lee Oskar).

The Parts of the Harmonica

Look at this picture of a basic, standard ten hole blues style harmonica, with labelled parts. Does yours look like this? It should.

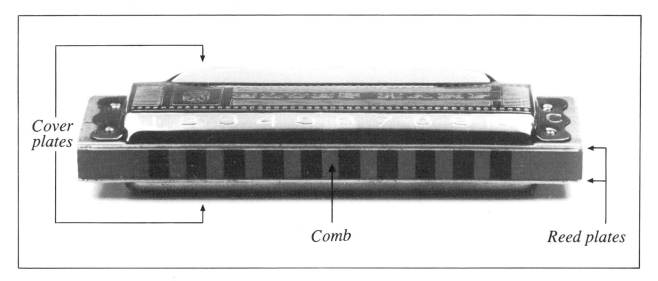

Cover plates

Comb *Reed plates*

What You Need to Know About The Holes

Your harmonica should feature ten holes, numbered from 1 to 10. Each hole contains two reeds, each of which vibrates to produce a particular sound called a note. One reed vibrates on the inhale, and the other vibrates on the exhale. Thus each hole provides two notes.

If you would like to know the letter names of the notes of the harmonica, please see Appendix B, on playing standard musical notation. An advanced harmonica technique, called bending, allows additional notes to be obtained. This technique is mostly used for blues, rock, and jazz music, and thus is explained in detail in the book *Progressive Blues Harmonica*.

Harmonica 'Keys'

Each of the brands and models discussed above is available in up to 12 different "keys". The term "key" refers both to the "Major Scale" that the harmonica is made to play, and to the lowest note of that particular harmonica. The Major Scale will be explained in greater detail in Lesson Eight.

Every harmonica has a small letter from "A" to "G" stamped on it, somewhere, to indicate its key. Some letters will be followed by a tiny "sharp" symbol (♯) or a tiny "flat" symbol (♭).

What You Need To know About Keys

Don't be intimidated by these little letters or symbols, even if you lack musical training or confidence. Surprisingly, the key of a harmonica makes very little difference to the beginning harmonica player! Although the "key of G" harp has a lower, heavier sound and the "key of F" harp a higher and more piercing tone, once you learn to play a harmonica in any key, you will be able to pick up and instantly play any other key harmonica.

Important: This book and the accompanying recording are intended for a harmonica in the key of "C".

The book will work perfectly well with any key harp, but the recording will only sound correct when played along with a "C" harmonica. Other than using a C harmonica, you do not need to worry any further about harmonica keys, for now.

Other Types Of Harmonicas

The larger "chromatic" harmonica, easily identifiable by its "slide button", is usually used for jazz and classical music, and is not appropriate for use with this book. Also, any harmonica whose holes are each split into two parts (the so-called "Echo" or "Tremolo" harmonicas) will be difficult to use with Section One of this book, and impossible to use with Section Two.

Lesson 2
Holding the Harmonica

There are many ways to hold a harmonica. Some people even use a mechanical device called a "rack" or "holder", which allows them to play "no hands" while strumming guitar or washing dishes. Bob Dylan is perhaps the best-known musician who plays using a rack.

The best way to hold the harmonica is as pictured, using the left hand, with the low numbered end of the harmonica butted gently between your thumb and forefinger. This hand position will prepare you to later use the sound effect known as the "hand vibrato", as explained in Lesson Nine. It can be used by right or left-handed players alike. Keep the four fingers of the left hand straight, and pressed gently but closely together, with no visible gaps between them.

The numbers from one to ten on the top cover of your harmonica should be clearly visible (if they are not, you are probably holding your instrument upside-down). The higher the number, the higher the sound of the two notes (in and out) which that numbered hole can produce. Don't squeeze the instrument too tightly, or your hand will get tired.

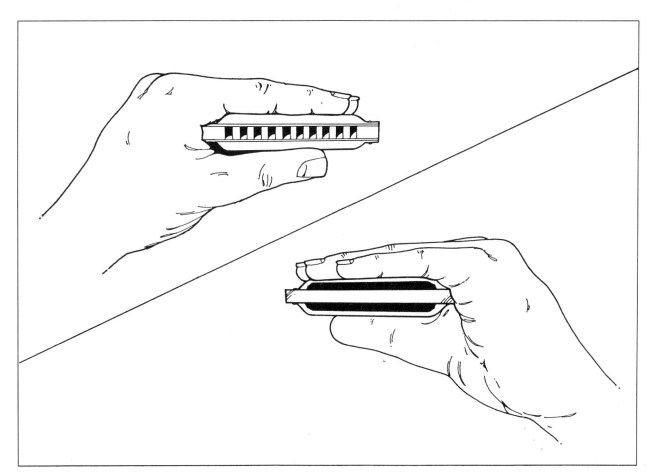

Mouthing The Harmonica: Low, Middle, and High

Cover a few of the low-end holes (such as the holes numbered 1, 2, and 3) with your mouth, and gently **exhale** air through the harmonica. The harp should be well into your mouth, that is, your upper lip must extend onto the top of the upper cover plate, and your lower lip under the bottom cover plate, as in the diagram. In this position, your lips may be slightly in contact with your forefinger on top and your thumb on bottom. **Inhale** on the low-end holes, also, to produce a different set of sounds.

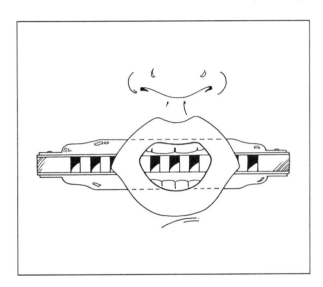 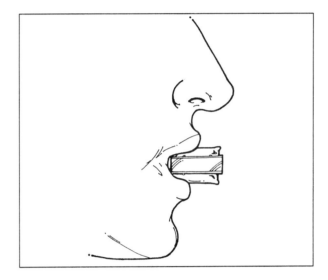

Cover some of the middle holes (such as the holes numbered 4, 5 and 6) with your mouth, and exhale and inhale here to produce two sets of slightly higher sounds.

Cover the highest holes (such as the holes numbered 8, 9, and 10) with your mouth, and exhale and inhale to produce two sets of high sounds.

A Random Inhale and Exhale Exercise

 Exercise 1

After experimenting with inhaling and exhaling on the low, middle, and high notes, keep your lips gently in place against the harmonica, and move the harmonica from side to side against your mouth while inhaling and exhaling at random. This will be simpler to do if you lightly wet your lips with your tongue first, to avoid friction. Attempt to keep your lips in the same formation that you used when covering three holes at a time, even as your harmonica is sliding through them.

How Much Air To Use

In general, send approximately as much breathe through the holes of the harmonica as you would use when talking at a normal voice level. Inhaling or exhaling very forcefully may shorten the life of the harmonica somewhat. You may notice that less air flow is required to produce the same volume of sound on the higher holes than is needed for the low or middle ones.

Conserving Air by Keeping the Nose Shut

You will find that you use less air when playing if you consciously direct all of your breath through your mouth, rather than through both nose and mouth simultaneously. Practice breathing through your mouth only for a moment if you need to, to concentrate on keeping the passage between nose and mouth shut tightly. Nose closure is especially important when doing the <u>inhaling</u> exercises, below.

Rhythm

The term "rhythm" can be used in a general or a specific manner. Generally, rhythm refers to the elements of time in music, such as the speed with which a song is played (also called the "tempo"), or the duration of any note. In a more specific vein, the term rhythm refers to particular timing patterns of notes in a piece of music, as in any one of a multitude of "blues rhythms", "rock and roll rhythms", "jazz rhythms", and so on.

The Beat

The term "beat" refers to the basic underlying pulse of a piece of music. When listening to a piece, most people will want to tap their feet at a particular speed. This is the beat of that piece of music. A beat is usually consistent, which means that the time passing between each beat remains precisely the same.

Tapping To The Beat

Tap your foot so that the amount of time between each tap is exactly the same. If this seems hard to do at first, walk at a very steady pace, observing that the time between each footfall remains the same. It may be easier to learn about this material by listening to the recorded accompaniment than by just reading about it.

Now count "one" "two" "three" "four" as you tap your foot. Say each number out loud, <u>exactly</u> as your foot hits the floor. Try to keep the time that passes between each tap precisely the same. You'll probably need to catch a very quick inhaled breath after each "four", without lengthening the time between that "four" and the following "one".

Your Basic Beat

Exercise 2

			(breathe)				
"one"	"two"	"three"	"four"	"one"	"two"	"three"	"four"
tap	**tap**	**tap**	**tap**	**tap**	**tap**	**tap**	**tap**

Once this feels familiar, do the same thing, but count only the beats "one", "two", and "three" out loud, and mouth the "four" beat silently. You can then catch your breath while the "four" tap is occurring.

Exercise 3

"one"	"two"	"three"	breathe	"one"	"two"	"three"	breathe
tap	**tap**	**tap**	**tap**	**tap**	**tap**	**tap**	**tap**

About The Count

It is customary to count a few beats before beginning a song or rhythm, in order to indicate the speed or tempo of the piece. Musicians call this the count or count-off. Most of the pieces in this book, as demonstrated on the recording, will be preceded by a count of four beats ("one, two, three, four") to prepare you for the beat of the song or rhythm. Occasionally, a count other than four (usually three) will be used, for reasons explained later in the text.

Lesson 3
Playing to the Basic Beat

Put your mouth over the middle holes (numbered 4, 5, and 6) of the harmonica, and continue to tap your foot steadily. Send a short exhaled breath of air through the harp, once for each count of "one", "two", "three", and "four". You may find it easier to actually <u>whisper</u> the words "one", "two", "three", and "four" right through the holes. Don't say the words aloud, or the vocal noise will obscure the harmonica sound.

You will probably find that you run out of air in short order, so drop the "four" as you did in the last exercise. In the place of actually saying the "four", use that time to swing the harmonica a fraction of an inch away from your lower lip, while keeping it in position against your upper lip, and breathe in. Return the harmonica to its original position in time for the next "one" beat. For now, don't inhale back through the harmonica on the count of "four", instead, remain silent during that beat. This is indicated by placing the (inhale) in brackets.

 Exercise 4
(exhaling through the 4, 5, and 6 holes)

"one"	"two"	"three"	(inhale)	"one"	"two"	"three"	(inhale)
tap	**tap**	**tap**	**tap**	**tap**	**tap**	**tap**	**tap**

The Bar or Measure

For your information, each individual "four tap's worth" of these rhythm patterns that you've been learning can be called one **"bar"** or one **"measure"**.

Some Less Basic Variations On Playing To The Beat

Now, for variety, rather than using three or four separate breaths of air to create three or four distinct sounds, try exhaling one long, steady breath through the harmonica that lasts all during the "one", "two" and "three" before inhaling silently during the count of "four". Remember to tap your foot steadily, and think the numbers to yourself while playing.

 **Exercise 5**
(through the 4, 5, and 6 holes)

exhale steadily on	these beats	(inhale)	exhale steadily on	these beats	(inhale)
tap tap tap		tap	tap tap tap		tap

Try breathing back in through the harmonica this time, on the "four" tap of each rhythm pattern. Use separate exhaled breaths of air for the "one", "two", and "three" taps. Keep tapping out a steady beat with your foot, and try all of these breathing exercises on the low and high-end holes as well as the middle.

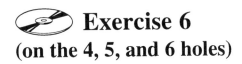 **Exercise 6**
(on the 4, 5, and 6 holes)

exhale	exhale	exhale	inhale	exhale	exhale	exhale	inhale
tap	tap	tap	tap	tap	tap	tap	tap

Staccato Effects: Puffing and Tonguing

The musical term "staccato" (from the Italian word for "detached") refers to notes that are clear and separate from each other. There are two ways to break up the airstream coming from your lungs into the harmonica so that it can be used to form a series of clear, distinct sounds. You can send separate short, exhaled puffs of air through the harmonica, as though you were trying to blow out a match sharply. Or you can use your <u>tongue</u> to break up the airstream, as you did when saying "one", "two" and "three" through the harp.

In general, tonguing is a more effective and versatile way to create separate sounds, so make sure that you practice it. Rather than saying "one", "two", or "three", try saying "ta-ta-ta" through the harmonica. Experiment with different sounds. You'll find that "cha-cha-cha" will produce a sound quite different from "da-da-da", "ba-ba-ba", "la-la-la", or "ka-ka-ka", as slightly different movements of the tongue are required to produce each syllable. Most harmonicists find "da", "ka", and "ta" sounds to be the easiest to use.

Inhaling Exercises

Tap your foot, and breathe in (nose closed) with your mouth covering the middle holes of the harmonica. Inhale during the 1, 2, and 3 counts, then swivel the harmonica a fraction of an inch away from your lower lip to exhale during the "four" count.

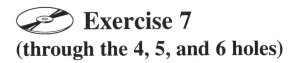 **Exercise 7**
(through the 4, 5, and 6 holes)

inhale steadily on	these beats		(exhale)	inhale steadily on	these beats		(exhale)
tap	**tap**	**tap**	**tap**	**tap**	**tap**	**tap**	**tap**

When this feels comfortable, try to take a separate short inhale **puff** for each "one", "two" and "three" count, plus a silent "four" to exhale during. Then try to make separate sounds by **tonguing** "da-ta-da" or "ta-ta-ta" while inhaling.

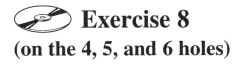 **Exercise 8**
(on the 4, 5, and 6 holes)

inhale	inhale	inhale	(exhale)	inhale	inhale	inhale	(exhale)
tap	**tap**	**tap**	**tap**	**tap**	**tap**	**tap**	**tap**

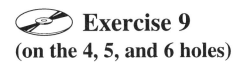 **Exercise 9**
(on the 4, 5, and 6 holes)

"ta"	"ta"	"ta"		"ta"	"ta"	"ta"	
inhale	inhale	inhale	(exhale)	inhale	inhale	inhale	(exhale)
tap	**tap**	**tap**	**tap**	**tap**	**tap**	**tap**	**tap**

Vary the above exercise by exhaling through the harmonica on the "four" beat. You may find that you need to make the one exhaled beat somewhat louder than the three inhaled beats, in order to rid yourself of excess air.

Exercise 10
(on the 4, 5, and 6 holes)

"ta"	"ta"	"ta"	"ta"	"ta"	"ta"	"ta"	"ta"
inhale	inhale	inhale	exhale	inhale	inhale	inhale	exhale
tap	tap	tap	tap	tap	tap	tap	tap

Tonguing on the inhale is somewhat harder than tonguing on the exhale, since exhale tonguing is much more similar to what we normally do when speaking. But our tongues are quick learners, and a few moments of slow, patient practice here will work wonders. Feel free to practice inhaling "da-ta-da" or "ta-ta-ta" <u>without</u> your harmonica for a bit, if that seems easier.

Two Points On Inhaled Notes:

There are two points that are essential to obtaining clear inhaled notes on the harmonica. You must breathe through the mouth only, and you must begin any inhaled exercise with sufficient air in the lungs.

Lesson 4
Harmonica Chords

Fortunately for the beginning student, the harmonica is constructed so that any two holes that are next to each other will produce sounds that go together well. Sounds that are produced by playing three or more holes simultaneously are called "chords". Each chord can be described by a letter name, like C, or F, or G, but these letter names are more of interest to guitarists and keyboard players than to harmonica players.

The most common number of holes used to play a chord is three. You have already been playing chords using the low-end holes 1, 2 and 3; the middle holes 4, 5 and 6, and the high-end holes 8, 9 and 10.

Three holes are the number most comfortable to cover without placing the teeth in contact with the harmonica (which you shouldn't be doing). If you are not sure how many holes you're covering at once, you might try using the very tip of your tongue to count holes, while your mouth is in position over them. Try to cover three, but your chord will still sound right if you cover four by accident, at first.

If You've Got An Accompanist, Or The Recording

Although most harmonica players, at this point in their careers, will be playing solo (by themselves), the small letters underneath many of the rhythm patterns and songs presented from now on will indicate the letter names of the chords that a guitarist or pianist might play to accompany that rhythm or song. These accompanying chords are the ones used in the *Progressive Harmonica* recording, and their importance will become more obvious in later lessons, with the study of blues, rock, and jazz improvisation.

A Simple Rhythm Pattern

This exercise sounds fairly good, and will help you to develop your breath control. It will also form the basis for your first train rhythm.

Place your mouth over the middle holes 4, 5, and 6. Tap your foot in the steady "one" "two" "three" "four" rhythm that you've already learned, slowly and carefully.

Inhale the chord twice (once for each foot tap), using either the "puffing" or "tonguing" methods of producing separate, repeated sounds. Then **Ex**hale the chord twice (once for each foot tap). Do this same four count chord rhythm over and over, as follows, just on the 4, 5, and 6 holes.

Once you get into the proper rhythm, there is no need to think about the "one" "two" "three" "four" any longer, because you will probably be able to maintain it without thinking. Below, **in** represents an inhaled chord and **ex** represents an exhaled chord.

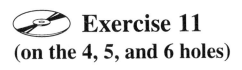 **Exercise 11**
(on the 4, 5, and 6 holes)

in	in	ex	ex	in	in	ex	ex
tap	tap	tap	tap	tap	tap	tap	tap
D		C		D		C	

Maintaining Enough Air Flow

Make sure that you are inhaling approximately the same amount of air that you are exhaling, so that you keep a comfortable amount of air in your lungs at all times. If you find yourself too full of air, exhale harder during the two exhaled chords. If you find yourself too empty, inhale harder during the two inhaled chords. Remember, keeping your nose closed will make more air available for playing, although at first it may be tempting to let air in or out of your nose to compensate for excess fullness or emptiness.

You do not need to play this rhythm pattern too loudly, especially at first. In fact, playing too hard may make you feel lightheaded. If this is a problem for you, just play very softly at first, using only as much air as feels comfortable.

Playing A Train Rhythm

The harmonica is particularly well-suited to mimic a railroad train. Thus a variety of train rhythms are part of the repertoire of every amateur and professional harmonicist. Although many train rhythms can be quite complex and difficult to play, even the simplest is entertaining and satisfying for the beginner.

When you are able to play the previous rhythm pattern, it can be altered to represent the sound of a moving train quite easily. Try it using a sharply tongued "chuck" for each out note, as follows.

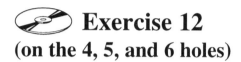 **Exercise 12**
(on the 4, 5, and 6 holes)

		"chuck"	"chuck"			"chuck"	"chuck"
in	in	ex	ex	in	in	ex	ex
tap	tap	tap	tap	tap	tap	tap	tap
D		C		D		C	

The chords represent the noise of the wheels, so simply change the tempo (speed) and volume (loudness) of the pattern to reflect the sound of a real train as it moves about. Make your rhythm pattern louder or softer, to mimic the noise of the train as it comes towards you or moves away from you. Speed the tempo up to represent the speed of the train increasing as it leaves a station or or slow the tempo down to represent the speed of the train decreasing as it approaches a station.

The Hardest Chord To Play: The 1, 2, and 3 Hole Inhale

You may want to begin playing the above train rhythm on the 1, 2 and 3 holes as well as on the 4, 5 and 6. Many beginning harmonica players find that the inhale of this lower chord tends to have a "choked" sound if there is the least bit of tension in the throat, tongue, or mouth. This is due to the tendency of the number 2 hole to "choke up" when inhaled. You will easily hear the difference between a "choked" and a "normal" sounding 1, 2 and 3 hole inhaled chord, as demonstrated on the recording.

Therefore, it is important to consciously relax the entire vocal apparatus when working on the 1, 2 and 3 inhale chord or the 2 inhale note. Thinking of the sensation of openness inside the mouth during a yawn may help this relaxation. The inhaled 1, 2 and 3 chord and 2 note are crucial to blues and rock playing, and thus well worth a minute or two of practice every day.

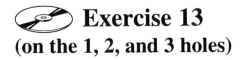 **Exercise 13**
(on the 1, 2, and 3 holes)

		"chuck"	"chuck"			"chuck"	"chuck"
in	in	ex	ex	in	in	ex	ex
tap	tap	tap	tap	tap	tap	tap	tap
G		C		G		C	

Lesson 5
About Single Notes: Read, But Don't Worry

Now that you have learned to use chords, it is time to begin working on isolating one hole at a time to produce a single note.

The sound produced by inhaling or exhaling on a single hole is called a "note", as opposed to the chord formed by inhaling or exhaling on more than one hole.

However, since chords may be used in the place of single notes for the entire first half of this book, you may want to simply read this Lesson, rather than spending a great deal of time practicing either of the two techniques for obtaining single notes.

Tongue-Blocking

Traditionally, harmonica players have used the method known as "tongue-blocking" to get single notes. This method involves covering four holes with the mouth, and then blocking the three leftmost holes with the side of the tongue. In the past, all beginners were forced to learn this difficult way of single-noting.

However, tongue-blocking, although essential for very serious classical harmonicists, is not really appropriate for those beginning students interested in playing mostly folk, blues, rock, or country music.

If you have already learned to get single notes in this way, please learn to also use the easier "pucker" method described below. If you can't tongue-block now, don't consider learning it now.

Eventually all serious or professional players will want to be able to obtain single notes both ways, but for beginners the pucker method is both simpler and more versatile.

A specialized form of tongue-blocking, known as "Octave-Blocking", lends a full, rich sound to the harmonica and is explained in the *Supplementary Songbook.*

The 'Pucker' Method of Single-Noting

Whistling, or drinking liquid through a straw, provides a mouth position similar to the mouth position needed to get single notes with the pucker method. Simply make a small hole with your mouth, approximately the same size as one hole on the harmonica. Tighten the muscles that circle your mouth to form a round, tight, hole as pictured.

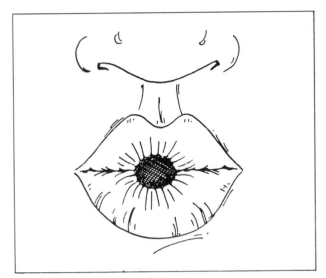

'Pucker' Method

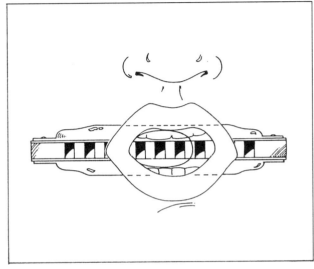

Tongue Blocking

Cover the number 1 hole of the harmonica with your "puckered" mouth. You should <u>not</u> be "reaching out" towards the harmonica with your lips. Instead, make sure that the harmonica is well <u>in between</u> your lips, with your upper lip well on top, and lower lip well beneath.

This will put the harmonica in contact with the wet, inner part of your lips, not the dry, outer parts. The muscle between the bottom of your nose and your upper lip should be shortened, as if you were curling your upper lip in an upwards direction. Gently exhale into the number 1 hole to produce a single note.

If you aren't sure that you're getting a single 1 note, you can put your finger over hole number 2. Although having to cover both the hole and your finger with your mouth may feel awkward, this will allow you to hear exactly what the single 1 hole note should sound like. Remove your finger, and try again.

After you've worked with exhaling on hole 1, try inhaling on it. Most people find the inhaled single notes harder at first. If you want to try something really difficult now, begin working on the single notes from holes 2 through 9. Holes 1 and 10 are the easiest, since they only have neighboring holes that must be avoided on one side.

Exercise 14

This exercise demonstrates what a the single notes from hole 1 and then hole 2 sound like, with the exhale played first, and then the inhale.

Getting single notes is not easy for most people, so don't allow yourself to become discouraged, or spend more than five or ten minutes on this today at most. Fortunately, all of the Part One material will work reasonably well even if you cannot obtain clear single notes at first.

Do keep practicing single-noting for a few minutes each day, and eventually you'll be able to get clear single notes when practicing. Of course, it is far simpler to locate and play a single note during a practice session than it is during a song. But as time passes, you will be able to locate just the note you want more and more often. The ability to consistently hit any single note at will can take months of diligent practice.

Lesson 6
About Written Notation Systems for the Harmonica

Most music instruction methods require the beginning student to learn the universal music notation system known as "standard notation". However, due to the fact that each ten hole or blues style harmonica is tuned to a particular key as discussed in Lesson One, standard notation is not a useful or appropriate system for us. Why this is so will be explained in the Music Theory and the Harmonica Appendix.

All of the different key harmonicas can be easily played by learning just one simple notation system. A number of slight variations on this system exist, but all effective harmonica notation systems include the following elements:

- an element that indicates which hole number to use
- an element that indicates whether to inhale or exhale
- an element that indicates how long to hold the note for

The Notation System Used In This Book

In the notation system used in the rest of this book:

- The <u>Numbers from 1-10</u> indicate which hole to use (refering to the numbers on top of the harmonica).
- The Letter "i" indicates an <u>i</u>nhaled Breath.
- The Letter "e" indicates an <u>e</u>xhaled Breath.

When writing the notes to a song or exercise, the hole number will be placed <u>above</u> the "i" or "e". For typographical convenience, when referring to a particular note in the text, the "i" or "e" will be placed <u>to the right</u> of the hole number.

For example, both **1̲_e** and **1e** mean: **e**xhale through the number **1** hole.

Similarly, both **3̲_i** and **3i** mean: **i**nhale through the number **3** hole.

With just a bit of practice, this system will become second nature to you. If you cannot answer the following questions, re-read this entire lesson from the beginning. What does **7i** mean? How about **4e**?

Chord Notation

Chords (notes that must be played all at one time) will be indicated by underlining them. So the rhythm of Lesson Three (in which we covered holes 4, 5 and 6 with our mouth, and played two inhaled chords and then two exhaled chords) would be notated like this:

<u>456</u>   <u>456</u>   <u>456</u>   <u>456</u>   <u>456</u>   <u>456</u>   <u>456</u>   <u>456</u>
 i   i   e   e   i   i   e   e

Just as with single notes, if it is necessary to refer to a chord in the text, it will be written out horizontally. So the chords used in the Train above would be written out as **<u>456</u>i** and **<u>456</u>e** respectively.

Timing Notation

The last part of our notation system is the timing slash. A timing slash shows you exactly when a tap of your foot should occur. For instance, in rhythm exercise number 11, you need to tap your foot once for each chord. Thus one timing slash appears above each chord. The distance between timing slashes has no effect on the timing (as illustrated in the song fragments in the following lesson), although whenever possible they will be kept uniformly distant.

Exercise 15

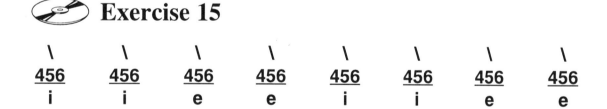

Tongueing Notation and Lyrics

If song lyrics or tongueing instructions are necessary, they will be placed above the timing slashes. For example, here is the train rhythm written in tablature.

Exercise 16

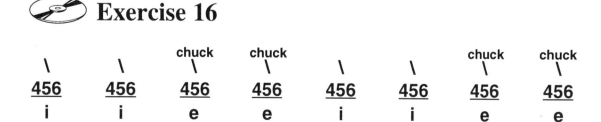

Lesson 7
Playing Songs And Rhythms From Notation

This notation system enables musicians to describe songs or rhythms clearly, so that other musicians can play them quickly and easily. Here is the notation that describes one possible variation of the Random Inhale and Exhale Exercise from Lesson Two without using words.

Try it, without worrying too much about landing on <u>precisely</u> the recommended chords. Attempt to do the exhales and inhales in the correct timing, with one beat per chord, and just use the low (123), middle (456), and high (789) chords.

Exercise 17

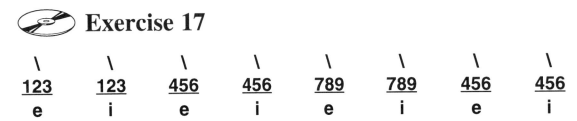

\	\	\	\	\	\	\	\
<u>123</u>	<u>123</u>	<u>456</u>	<u>456</u>	<u>789</u>	<u>789</u>	<u>456</u>	<u>456</u>
e	i	e	i	e	i	e	i

Following are the first few notes of some favorite songs that illustrate certain notation issues. Make sure that you understand the notation system, and if you like, play these examples. The complete songs will be presented further on in the text.

Notation For Holding Notes For More Than One Beat, and Other Complications

The first part of *Jingle Bells* can be notated so that the first two notes are held for one beat, and the third note for two beats, as indicated by the number of slashes above each note. This is then repeated.

Since you may not have mastered single noting, instead of using the note **5e**, you can instead use the chord **<u>456</u>e** that is centered around the desired **5e** note. However, from now on, the notation will be written *as though* you were able to use single notes. So, if necessary, look at the notation to determine the desired single note, then use the chord centered around that single note. The rest of this song, which does require use of notes other than the **5e**, can be found on page 63.

Exercise 18

\	\	\\	\	\	\\	(or more realistically)	\	\	\\
Jin	gle	bells	jin	gle	bells		jin	gle	bells
5	5	5	5	5	5		**456**	**456**	**456**
e	e	e	e	e	e		e	e	e

In the first line of *Twinkle Twinkle Little Star*, the initial jump from the 4 hole to the 6 may be a challenge. Practice the **4e** to **6e** jump separately for a moment, before playing. Use the **345e** and **567e** chords if you cannot obtain the single notes. Notice the inhaled notes under the word 'lit-tle'. The balance of this song is on page 31.

Exercise 19

Practice: 4 4 6 6   or   **345** **345** **567** **567**
            e e e e   e   e   e   e

Exercise 20

\	\	\	\	\	\	\\
Twin	kle	Twin	kle	Lit	tle	Star
4	4	6	6	6	6	6
e	e	e	e	i	i	e

When playing *Twinkle Twinkle Little Star*, and any other song, you have the choice of playing each note with a separate breath or puff of air, as described in the Staccato Effects section of Lesson Two. Or you can move smoothly from note to note, gently stopping and starting your breath to play the different notes (like the two beginning 4e notes), but without the sharpness that comes from using a puffing or tongueing effect.

In the traditional Afro-American song, *Oh When The Saints Go Marching In*, certain notes last for many beats. If you run out of air on the long notes, the version of *Saints* following this one may be more to your liking. The rest of this song is on page 32.

Exercise 21

\	\	\	\\\\\	\	\	\	\\\\\
Oh	when	the	saints	Go	mar	chin'	in
4	5	5	6	4	5	5	6
e	e	i	e	e	e	i	e

Notation For Silent Beats

Often songs have rests, which are beats or partial beats of silence. In this notation system, a rest is indicated by a timing slash which has no note written under it. This version of *Oh When The Saints Go Marching In* with rests may be easier on your lungs than the former version. Use the rest after the long **6e** to expel some breath while you locate the following note **4e**.

Exercise 22

\	\	\	\\\\	\
Oh	when	the	saints	(rest)
4	5	5	6	
e	e	i	e	

\	\	\	\\\\	\
Go	mar	chin'	in	(rest)
4	5	5	6	
e	e	i	e	

Lesson 8
About The Major Scale

The Major Scale provides the notes used in many of the world's best-known songs. You are probably already familiar with it, in the vocal form:

DO   RE   MI   FA   SO   LA   TI   DO.

The Major Scale is quite easy to play on the harmonica. In fact, the harmonica was originally constructed so that Major Scales and Major Chords would be very accessible.

Since you have a key of C harmonica, you will be playing a C Major Scale, that is, a Major Scale beginning and ending on the C note. This may also be called a Major Scale in the key of C. Major Scales in keys other than C can be played on the C harmonica, once the technique of bending is mastered, but they are far more difficult than the C Major Scale.

If you had a key of D harmonica, playing the notes written below in harmonica tablature would produce a D Major Scale. Likewise, if you had a B♭ (B flat) harmonica, playing the notes written on page 30 would produce a B♭ Major Scale.

Finding The First Note and Moving to the Next

You will probably not be able to play the C Major Scale using single notes yet. However, try to <u>center</u> your mouth on the correct hole, even if you have to let the neighboring holes on each side in as well. You will then be playing a chord version of a Major Scale, which will still be quite recognizable. Use the tip of your tongue to locate the number 1 hole, then count up, hole by hole, to the number 4 hole. Once you have located the 4 hole with your tongue-tip, pucker your mouth around your tongue, then retract your tongue, and your lips will be centered on the 4 hole.

Using your tongue-tip to investigate the distance between holes will help you to move accurately from one hole to the next. Try not to move <u>too far</u>, or you'll skip over the hole you want. But do make sure that you move <u>far enough</u>, so that you don't accidentally play the same hole twice, instead of moving on to the next. A few moments of tongue-tip location practice before attempting the Major Scale may really help you to learn the distance between holes.

Playing The Major Scale

This is the easiest Major Scale to play on the harmonica, although not the only one. Remember: **i** means **inhale, e** means **exhale**. Note that the **e i - e i - e i** pattern of the holes of the Major Scale changes as you go from the 6 hole (e i) to the 7 hole (i e). Since no timing slashes are indicated, you may play the notes along with foot taps or not, as you prefer.

💿 Exercise 23

The Major Scale:	4	4	5	5	6	6	7	7
	e	i	e	i	e	i	i	e

💿 Exercise 24

The Major Scale: (chord version)	345	345	456	456	567	567	678	678
	e	i	e	i	e	i	i	e

Playing The Reverse Major Scale

Your ability to play songs will be increased if you also practice playing the Major Scale from high end to low.

💿 Exercise 25

Reverse Major Scale:	7	7	6	6	5	5	4	4
	e	i	i	e	i	e	i	e

📖1 Using the *Supplementary Songbook*

You are now ready to begin to play the songs in Part One of the *Progressive Harmonica Supplementary Songbook*, as described on page 78.

Twinkle Twinkle Little Star - 1

Practice the Major Scales for a few moments, and then try the following song in its entirety. Once again, if the single notes as written seem too hard to strive for, just try to center your mouth on the note that is written, and don't worry if the notes on either side of it "creep in" a little. All of the Part One material can be played perfectly well, even if you cannot yet get single notes.

\	\	\	\	\	\	\\		\	\	\	\	\	\	\\
Twin	kle	twin	kle	lit	tle	star		How	I	won	der	what	you	are
4	4	6	6	6	6	6		5	5	5	5	4	4	4
e	e	e	e	i	i	e		i	i	e	e	i	i	e
C				F		C		F		C		G		C

\	\	\	\	\	\	\\		\	\	\	\	\	\	\\
Up	a	bove	the	world	so	high		Like	a	dia	mond	in	the	sky
6	6	5	5	5	5	4		6	6	5	5	5	5	4
e	e	i	i	e	e	i		e	e	i	i	e	e	i
C		F		C		G		C		F		C		G

\	\	\	\	\	\	\\		\	\	\	\	\	\	\\
Twin	kle	twin	kle	lit	tle	star		How	I	won	der	what	you	are
4	4	6	6	6	6	6		5	5	5	5	4	4	4
e	e	e	e	i	i	e		i	i	e	e	i	i	e
C				F		C		F		C		G		C

Oh When The Saints Go Marching In

In this song, you can play the long notes in either of two ways. For instance, you can play the **6e** note under "saints" as one long, four beat note, or as four separate one beat notes, each created by a separate tonguing or puffing effect. Do whichever you prefer, or alternate.

Before beginning the song, notice portions which may be difficult, such as the part in the third line which requires nine beats of exhale in a row. Make sure to inhale enthusiastically on the single inhaled note preceding the nine exhaled notes.

\	\	\	\\\\	\	\	\	\	\\\\	\
Oh	when	the	saints		go	mar	chin'	in	
4	5	5	6		4	5	5	6	
e	e	i	e		e	e	i	e	
C									

\	\	\	\\	\\	\\	\\	\\\\	\\
Oh	when	the	saints	go	mar	chin'	in	
4	5	5	6	5	4	5	4	
e	e	i	e	e	e	e	i	
							G	

\	\	\\\	\	\\	\	\	\	\\\\	\
Yes	I	want	to	be	in	that	num	ber	
5	4	4	4	5	6	6	6	5	
e	i	e	e	e	e	e	e	i	
		C						F	

\	\	\\	\\	\\	\\	\\\\	\
When	the	saints	go	mar	chin'	in	
5	5	6	5	4	4	4	
e	i	e	e	e	i	e	
		C		G		C	

Lesson 9
More Simple Songs With One Note Per Beat

The following songs can all be notated so that no more than one note occurs per beat, although other timing versions may be more commonly used, as demonstrated at the end of Lesson Twelve.

These songs will sound correct if played using chords centered on the single note that is written, but continue to work on obtaining single notes as well as possible. You may wish to practice using the hand vibrato on the notes that are held for multiple beats, as described at the end of this lesson.

Some Tonal Variations

Please note that although the following songs are all notated *entirely* with single notes, it is sometimes acceptable to use a combination of single notes as well as chords when playing them. Some songs may sound better when played with a greater number of chords in place of single notes, others may sound better when played with more single notes. Thus if a song uses the single note **4e**, it may also be played as the chord **345e**, or as **34e** or **45e**. This choice is up to you.

When a song "jumps" from one note to a distant note (as with the jump from **4e** to **6e** in *Twinkle Twinkle Little Star*), it is acceptable to jump directly from the 4 to the 6 hole, or to "slide" the harmonica, briefly hitting upon the 5 hole. However, the slide must not interfere with the correct timing of the song. It is also acceptable either to use, or not to use, a tonguing effect on any note or chord. Unless notated, this is entirely left to your discretion, depending on whether you prefer a "flowing" (not tongued) or "sharp" version of the song. All of these variations are demonstrated on the recording, used appropriately depending on the song.

For He's A Jolly Good Fellow

This good-natured song, like *On Top Of Old Smoky* which follows, is usually notated so that each beat has up to three notes, as it has been presented at the end of Lesson Fourteen. But it is easier to read when written like this.

\	\\	\	\	\	\	\\\	\	\
For	he's	a	jol	ly	good	fel	low	
4	5	5	5	4	5	5	5	
e	e	e	e	i	e	i	e	
C						F	C	

\	\\	\	\	\	\	\\\	\	\
For	he's	a	jol	ly	good	fel	low	
5	4	4	4	4	4	5	4	
e	i	i	i	e	i	e	e	
	G					C		

\	\\	\	\	\	\	\\\	\	\
For	he's	a	jol	ly	good	fel	low	
4	5	5	5	4	5	5	6	
e	e	e	e	i	e	i	i	
						F		

\	\	\	\	\\	\	\	\\\\
That	no	bod	y	can	de	ny	
6	6	6	6	5	4	4	
i	e	i	e	i	i	e	
	C			G		C	

\	\	\	\	\\	\	\	\\\\
That	no	bod	y	can	de	ny	
5	6	6	6	6	6	6	
e	e	e	e	i	i	e	
				F		C	

\	\	\	\	\\	\	\	\\\\
That	no	bod	y	can	de	ny	
6	5	5	5	5	5	5	
e	e	e	e	i	i	e	
				F		C	

\	\\	\	\	\	\	\\\	\	\
For	he's	a	jol	ly	good	fel	low	
4	5	5	5	4	5	5	6	
e	e	e	e	i	e	i	i	
						F		

\	\	\	\	\\	\	\	\\\\
That	no	bod	y	can	de	ny	
6	6	6	6	5	4	4	
i	e	i	e	i	i	e	
	C			G		C	

🎵 On Top Of Old Smoky

\	\	\	\	\\\	\\\	\\	\	\	\	\	\\\	\\\	\\
On	top	of	old	Smo	ky		all	co	vered	with	snow		
4	4	5	6	7	6		6	5	6	6	6		
e	e	e	e	e	i		i	i	e	i	e		
C				F						C			

\	\	\	\	\\\	\\\	\\	\	\	\	\	\\\	\\\	\\
I	lost	my	true	lov	er		a	court	'in	too	slow		
4	4	5	6	6	4		5	5	5	4	4		
e	e	e	e	e	i		e	i	e	i	e		
				G						C			

The Hand Vibrato

By using the right hand to form an enclosure around the left hand and the harmonica, an effect known as the hand vibrato is made possible by opening and closing the right hand. Harmonica players sometimes refer to this effect as the "wah wah" or "hand wah wah".

Hold the harmonica in the left hand as described at the beginning of Lesson Two, with the fingers of the left hand straight and pressed together, with no visible gaps between them. Place the heel of the right hand against the heel of the left hand, so that the flattened right palm covers the "cup" formed by the left hand as it holds the harmonica.

The hand position, with the cup closed, is somewhat like one that could be used to carry water in the absence of a glass, with the fingers of the left hand curled inside the fingers of the right, and the left pinky pushed against the right hand where the fingers join the palm.

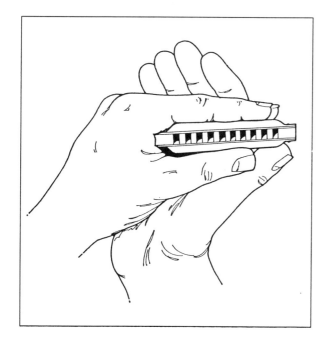
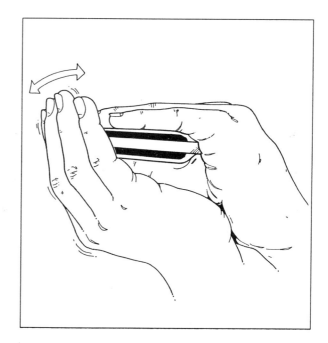

The point of this hand position is to be able to block and unblock the flow of air through the harmonica. As hands come in varying shapes and sizes, experiment with the right hand position that will most comfortably block the air flow. It may be useful to look into a mirror, to see how well the right hand closes about the left.

Practicing The Hand Vibrato

Begin in closed hand position. Keeping the heels of the hands together, bend the right hand back from the wrist so that the "cup" opens, then close it. You need only open the "cup" an inch or less to change the sound. Experiment with both inhaled and exhaled single notes and chords, on the high, middle, and low parts of the harmonica. The lower or middle notes will generally produce a more pronounced wah wah, at first. Practice opening and closing the "cup" once per beat, as in this pattern.

Exercise 26

```
wah     wah     wah             wah     wah     wah
 \       \       \       \       \       \       \       \
123     123     123             123     123     123
 e       e       e               e       e       e
```

Practice also opening and closing the cup in a smooth, fluttering motion, as swiftly as possible.

Using The Hand Vibrato

The hand vibrato can be used in many ways. Opening and closing once per note, on notes that are held for one beat, will emphasize the clarity of each note. Doing a continuous fast (fluttering) hand vibrato throughout a song, or portion of a song, will provide a pleasant tonal effect that is easily over-used.

It is wiser to use a fluttering hand vibrato only on selected notes that are held for multiple beats, such as the long note or notes at the end of each line of *On Top Of Old Smoky*. When using this faster wah wah during a song, it is important not to lose the beat.

Lesson 10
About The Alternate Major Scales

Although the C Major Scale that runs between the notes **4e** and **7e** is the easiest one to play on the harmonica, it is not the only one. There are two other C Major Scales available. However, each one is missing notes that must be supplied by either the advanced technique known as 'bending' or buy the somewhat easier technique called "octave note substitution".

Octave notes are notes that have the same letter name. They sound very much alike, even though there is a difference in pitch (the highness or lowness of a note).

In the following chart of the notes available without bending on the C harmonica, you will see four C notes, four G notes, three D and E notes, and two F, A and B notes. Any note with the same letter name may be substituted for any other note with the same letter name.

C	D	E	G	G	B	C	D	E	F	G	A	B	C	D	E	F	G	A	C
1	1	2	2	3	3	4	4	5	5	6	6	7	7	8	8	9	9	10	10
e	i	e	i	e	i	e	i	e	i	e	i	i	e	i	e	i	e	i	e

A moment's practice playing the various C notes will be well worthwhile.

💿 Exercise 27

C	C	C	C	C	C	C	C
1	4	7	10	10	7	4	1
e	e	e	e	e	e	e	e

What The Alternate Major Scales Are Missing

As the above chart shows, only the middle holes 4 through 7 can produce an entire C Major Scale: C D E F G A B C. In the holes 1 through 4, the F and A notes have been omitted, and the G note doubled. This makes certain chords easier to play, and the low C Major Scale very difficult to play without extensive bending.

In the holes 7 through 10, an almost complete C Major Scale can be played, with the exception of the missing note B. Since only one note is missing, and that note near the end of the scale, octave substitution can be used to complete this high Major Scale.

If you are daring, you may choose to play the songs in Lesson Eleven without practicing the following scales. The scales are somewhat less entertaining than the songs, but will make the songs easier to play, and explain why the alternate versions of certain songs work.

The High Major Scale

Try playing the high C Major Scales, by simply skipping the missing B note. Perhaps you will be able to "hear it in your mind" while passing it over. If not, the substitution exercises below will allow you to complete these useful scales.

Exercise 28

High Major Scale:	C	D	E	F	G	A	(B)	C
	7	8	8	9	9	10	X	10
	e	i	e	i	e	i	X	e

Exercise 29

Reverse High Major Scale:	C	(B)	A	G	F	E	D	C
	10	X	10	9	9	8	8	7
	e	X	I	E	I	E	I	E

Playing Major Scales With The Simplest Octave Substitutions

By substituting octave notes, the high C Major Scale can be completed. But before attempting to do so, first practice the C Major Scale as learned in Lesson Eight, and some simpler substitutions.

Exercise 30

4	4	5	5	6	6	7	7
e	i	e	i	e	i	i	e

Then play it with the simplest octave note substitutions, which involve replacing the 7e with a 10e or a 1e.

Exercise 31

4	4	5	5	6	6	7	10
e	i	e	i	e	i	i	e

Exercise 32

4	4	5	5	6	6	7	1
e	i	e	i	e	i	i	e

Playing Reverse Major Scales With The Simplest Octave Substitutions

These scales do not have to be mastered in order to play most of the songs in this book, but attempting to do so will provide good practice for locating notes that are not near each other.

Exercise 33

7	7	6	6	5	5	1	1
e	i	i	e	i	e	i	e

Exercise 34

7	7	6	6	5	2	1	1
e	i	i	e	i	e	i	e

The High Major Scales With Octave Substitutions

Playing these scales will make the high portions of the songs in Lesson Eleven easy to play. A moment of practice going from the 7 to the 10 hole will help a great deal before playing the scales. The reversed high Major Scale is easier than the other, since jumping from hole 7 to hole 10 is easier than vice versa.

Exercise 35

7	7	10	9	9	8	8	7
e	i	i	e	i	e	i	e

Exercise 36

7	8	8	9	9	10	7	7
e	i	e	i	e	i	i	e

Lesson 11
More Songs

Good King Wenceslaus

This song uses many notes from the high Major Scale. It should not be played rapidly, nor generally can it be.

	\	\	\	\	\	\	\\	\	\	\	\	\\	\	\
	Good	king	Wen	ce	slas	look'd	out	On	the	feast	of	Ste	phen	
	7	7	7	8	7	7	6	6	6	6	7	7	7	
	e	e	e	i	e	e	e	i	e	i	i	e	e	
	C							F				C		

	\	\	\	\	\	\	\\	\	\	\	\	\\	\	\
	When	the	snow	lay	all	a	bout	deep	and	crisp	and	e	ven	
	7	7	7	8	7	7	6	6	6	6	7	7	7	
	e	e	e	i	e	e	e	i	e	i	i	e	e	
								F				C		

	\	\	\	\	\	\	\\	\	\	\	\	\\	\	\
	Bright	ly	shown	the	moon	that	night	tho'	the	frost	was	cru	el	
	9	9	8	8	8	8	7	6	6	6	7	7	7	
	e	i	e	i	e	i	e	i	e	i	i	e	e	
								F				C		

	\	\	\	\	\	\	\\	\	\	\	\\	\\	\\\	\
	When	a	poor	man	came	in	sight	gath	ring	win	ter	fu	u	el
	6	6	6	7	7	7	8	9	9	8	8	7	9	7
	e	e	i	i	e	e	i	e	i	e	i	e	i	e
						D	C					F	C	

♪2 Supplementary Songbook: Part Two

You are now ready to begin to play the songs in the *Progressive Harmonica Supplementary Songbook*, Part Two.

Red River Valley

Many octave substitutions can be made in this song. But without using any of them, the last line would require bending a note to supply the missing A note in the low Major Scale.

Two possible variations on the last line are notated. Either will work quite well, and delay the need for bending technique. The first ending jumps from the **6e** to the **3i** to stay mostly in the middle Major Scale, while the second ending ends the song in the high Major Scale. Both versions are demonstrated on the recording.

Use of the fluttering hand vibrato is practically a requirement on this song. Begin by applying it to the long note at the end of each line, then try to use it on any note held for two beats or more.

```
 \      \     \\    \     \     \\    \     \     \     \\\\   \
From   this   val   ley  they   say   you   are   go   ing
 3      4     5     5     4     4     4     5     4     4
 e      e     e     e     i     e     i     e     i     e
 C


 \      \     \\    \     \     \\    \     \     \\\   \\\
 We    will  miss  your bright eyes  and  sweet smile
 3      4     5     4     5     6     5     5     4
 e      e     e     e     e     e     i     e     i
                                                       G


 \      \     \\    \     \     \\    \     \     \     \\\\   \
But     re   mem   ber   the   Red   Ri    ver   Val   ley
 6      5     5     5     4     4     4     5     6     5
 e      i     e     e     i     e     i     e     e     i
              C                                   F


 \      \     \  \  \     \\    \     \     \\\   \\\
And    the   cow  boy   that  loved  you   so   true
 6      6     6    3     4     4     5     4     4
 i      i     e    i     e     i     e     i     e
              C          G                       C
```

or, substitute this last line

```
 \      \     \\    \     \     \\    \     \     \\\   \\\
And    the   cow   boy  that  loved  you   so   true
 6      6     6     7     7     8     8     8     7
 i      i     e     i     e     i     e     i     e
```

Amazing Grace

The first version of this lovely song uses many high Major Scale notes. The second version manages to stay mostly in the middle Major Scale by substituting the A note provided by 6i for the missing lower A. It sounds somewhat "jumpy", but is less shrill than the first one. You may wish to experiment with using one hand wah per beat, on all or some of the notes.

\	\\	\	\\	\	\\	\	\\	\	\\	\	\\	\	\\	\	\\	\\\
A	maz	ing	grace	how	sweet	the	sound	to	save	a	wretch	like	me			
6	7	8	8	8	7	6	6	6	7	8	8	8	9			
e	e	e	e	i	e	i	e	e	e	e	e	i	e			
C					F		C						G			

\	\\	\	\\	\	\\	\	\\	\	\\	\	\\	\	\\\	\\
I	once	was	lost	but	now	am	found	was	blind	but	now	can	see	
8	9	7	8	8	7	6	6	7	7	8	8	8	7	
e	e	e	e	i	e	i	e	e	e	e	e	i	e	
	C				F		C				G		C	

or

\	\\	\	\\	\	\\	\	\\	\	\\	\	\\	\	\\	\\\
A	maz	ing	grace	how	sweet	the	sound	to	save	a	wretch	like	me	
3	4	5	5	4	4	6	6	3	4	5	5	4	6	
e	e	e	e	i	e	i	e	e	e	e	e	i	e	
C					F		C						G	

\	\\	\	\\	\	\\	\	\\	\	\\	\	\\	\	\\\	\\
I	once	was	lost	but	now	am	found	was	blind	but	now	can	see	
5	6	4	5	4	4	6	6	3	4	5	5	4	4	
e	e	e	e	i	e	i	e	e	e	e	e	i	e	
	C				F		C				G		C	

The Repeat Sign

The repeat sign :|| tells the reader to repeat the entire piece preceding it. When used at the end of a song, repeat the entire song. When used at the end of a line that is not at the end of a song, repeat only the line preceding the repeat sign. This useful symbol will be used from now on.

Lesson 12
About Improvisation

Under each song and rhythm pattern are printed the letter names of the chords that can be used to accompany that piece. These particular chords are used because the notes of the song or the rhythm pattern fit in well with the notes of the chord.

When a harmonica player is playing a particular song, especially one that he or she knows well, the notes of the song are of primary importance, for it is the specific arrangement of the notes that makes a song recognizable. Although playing along to a chord accompaniment may make for a richer, fuller sound, it is not necessary.

Some types of music are not so much based on a specific arrangement of notes (which is called a melody, or tune). Instead, styles of music such as blues, jazz, and rock are often "improvised".

Improvisation is the act of creating music as it is being played. Unlike playing a specific song with its specified notes, this way of playing offers the musician a great deal of freedom in choosing the notes. However, the notes used in improvisation are far from randomly chosen. Improvisation will be covered, not in this book, but in *Progressive Blues Harmonica*, since it is in blues, rock, and jazz music that improvisation plays an essential part.

In order to give themselves a certain degree of order or organization, improvising musicians often play along with an accompaniment of chords. Thus they have a structure upon which to base their improvisations, and often allow their choice of notes to be determined by their knowledge of which notes will fit in well with those chords.

About The Twelve Bar Chord Structure

Most blues, many rock, and some jazz styles of music are heavily based on a particular repeated series of chords called "The Twelve Bar Chord Structure". Literally thousands of well known blues, rock, and jazz songs use just this one structure, also known as the Twelve Bar Progression or the Twelve Bar Blues Structure, which you will play in a moment.

Playing A Twelve Bar Chord Structure in G on the C Harmonica

As discussed in Lesson Five, it is easiest to play a Major Scale in the key of C, that is, a C Major Scale, on the C harmonica, although Major Scales in other keys may be played once bending is mastered.

Similarly, it is easiest to play blues on the C harmonica in the key of G, although other key blues are possible for the advanced player. Playing in the key of G on a C harmonica is known as playing "second position" harmonica, or "cross harp". The chart below describes the how the G chord, C chord, and D chord are used to play a Twelve Bar Chord Structure in the key of G. Each "bar", or four beat segment, is separated by a "bar line".

Notice that four beats of D chord are played at the end of the verse. These final beats of D chord are known as the "turnaround", for they are used in order to indicate that a verse is about to come to an end, and the next verse is about to begin. The turnaround may be only two or three beats of D instead of four, or it may be omitted entirely. If the (D) turnaround is less than four beats long, G chord beats will replace the "missing" D beats, so that the entire verse remains 48 beats, or 12 bars, long.

💿 Twelve Bar Chord Structure In The Key Of G

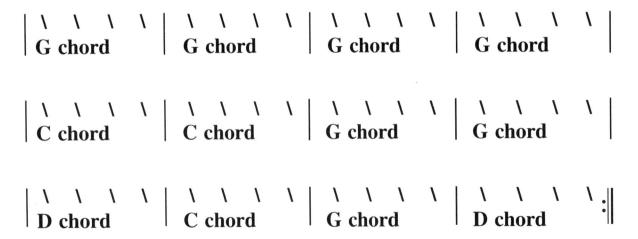

In Lesson Thirteen, an entire twelve bar blues structure of this type will be presented, as well as two more exciting variations on the twelve bar blues.

SECTION TWO

The ability to obtain single notes becomes more important in the second half of this book. Please return to Lesson Five and begin to practice this skill, if you have not already done so.

Lesson 13
The Cross Town Twelve Bar Blues

This is the simplest way to play a Twelve Bar Chord Structure in the key of G. Play it over and over, as per the repeat sign at the end of the entire twelve bars, until you can change chords at the correct time without looking at the notation.

The partial chord **45i** has been used for the D chord. It sounds crisper than the **345i**. You may find it worthwhile to practice the jump from the **123i** to the **45i** for a moment, before playing the entire piece.

Remember that one bar equals four beats, so that the term Twelve Bar refers to the length of one verse of this structure, as you can clearly see below. Instead of only indicating where the chords change, as has been done with the other songs in the book, in this piece the chord used in each bar has been indicated. This will help you to relate this piece to the chart on page 44, bar by bar. Notice the three beat turnaround, which includes two beats of D chord and one silent beat.

 ## The Cross Town Twelve Bar Blues

```
| \   \   \    \ | \   \   \    \ | \   \   \    \ | \   \   \    \ |
| 123 123 123   | 123 123 123   | 123 123 123   | 123 123 123   |
|  i   i   i    |  i   i   i    |  i   i   i    |  i   i   i    |
|  G            |  G            |  G            |  G            |

| \   \   \    \ | \   \   \    \ | \   \   \    \ | \   \   \    \ |
| 456 456 456   | 456 456 456   | 123 123 123   | 123 123 123   |
|  e   e   e    |  e   e   e    |  i   i   i    |  i   i   i    |
|  C            |  C            |  G            |  G            |

| \   \   \    \ | \   \   \    \ | \   \   \    \ | \   \   \    \ |
| 45  45  45    | 45  45  45    | 123 123 123   | 123 45  45    |:||
|  i   i   i    |  e   e   e    |  i   i   i    |  i   i   i    |
|  D            |  C            |  G            |  G   D        |
```

Other Harmonica Positions: First and Third

It is possible, although not as easy, to play blues on a C harmonica in keys other than G. Less convenient and popular but still common is the playing of C blues on a C harmonica. This is known as playing in "First Position", or "Straight Harp".

The least usual way to play blues that is still commonly heard is to play D blues on a C harmonica. This is known as playing in "Third Position". It is also occasionally referred to as "slant harp", and probably accounts for less than five percent of all blues played.

Although further discussion of either of these enjoyable and challenging ways of playing blues harmonica is beyond the scope of this book, they are covered in more detail in *Progressive Blues Harmonica*.

The Cross Town Arpeggiated Twelve Bar Blues

Rather than playing the three notes of each chord together, as above, in the following Twelve Bar Structure each note of the chord is played separately. Playing a chord in this way is known as "arpeggiating" a chord. This verse also features a full four beats of turnaround (including the final silent beat). By now, you should be working seriously on your ability to obtain single notes, if you cannot already do so.

\ \ \ \	\ \ \ \	\ \ \ \	\ \ \ \
1 2 3	1 2 3	1 2 3	1 2 3
i i i	i i i	i i i	i i i
G	G	G	G

\ \ \ \	\ \ \ \	\ \ \ \	\ \ \ \
4 5 6	4 5 6	1 2 3	1 2 3
e e e	e e e	i i i	i i i
C	C	G	G

\ \ \ \	\ \ \ \	\ \ \ \	\ \ \ \
4 5 6	4 5 6	1 2 3	4 5 6
i i i	e e e	i i i	i i i
D	C	G	D

The Basic Boogie Woogie

A boogie woogie is a particular type of Twelve Bar structure. Originally based on the notes played by the left hand of New Orleans style piano players in the early part of this century, it has been adapted into a standard harmonica piece.

It is more difficult to recognize the Twelve Bar Structure in the boogie woogie than in the previous blues pieces, but a careful count of the beats will prove that the chord changes are less obvious but do occur in the correct places. Be prepared for the turnaround, which requires a jump from **6e** to **1i**.

```
| \  \  \  \ | \  \  \  \ | \  \  \  \ | \  \  \  \ |
| 2  3  4  5 | 5  5  4    | 2  3  4  5 | 5  5  4    |
| i  i  i  e | i  e  i    | i  i  i  e | i  e  i    |
| G          | G          | G          | G          |

| \  \  \  \ | \  \  \  \ | \  \  \  \ | \  \  \  \ |
| 4  5  6  6 | 7  6  6    | 2  3  4  5 | 6  5  4    |
| e  e  e  i | e  i  e    | i  i  i  e | e  e  i    |
| C          | C          | G          | G          |

| \  \  \  \ | \  \  \  \ | \  \  \  \ | \  \  \  \ |
| 4  5  6  5 | 4  5  6  5 | 2  3  4  5 | 6  1  1    |
| i  i  i  i | e  e  e  e | i  i  i  e | e  i  i    |
| D          | C          | G          | G  D       |
```

Lesson 14
More Rhythm: Breaking Beats Into Parts

Beats are not the smallest timing units in music, since even single beats can be divided up into smaller parts. Take a moment and review the "one" "two" "three" "four" rhythm learned in Lesson Two. As you did then, say "One" "Two" "Three" "Four" while you tap your foot. This time, observe your foot very closely.

Notice that your foot raises itself up off the floor in between each tap. Since it is common for a note of a song to be played for less than one entire beat, it is important for musicians to be able to divide beats up into parts.

The most usual way for musicians to count a beat that is broken into two parts is to say: "One *and* Two *and* Three *and* Four *and*" instead of the usual "one" "two" "three" "four". You should be saying each "and" while your foot is in mid-air, between taps. If you refrain from saying "and" after the "four", you will have just enough time to catch a quick breath before beginning on "one" again.

Practice saying this new rhythm for a while, which can be notated like this. Notice that the beat, as indicated by the timing slash, falls on the numbers "one", "two", "three", and "four", which represent the actual taps of your foot on the floor. The "ands" occur in between the slashes, and represent the time that your foot is raised in between taps.

💿 Exercise 37

Playing The Doublet Rhythm Pattern

Play the rhythm as either a chord or single note, as you prefer. Use a "ta", "da", or "ka" tonguing to break the note into two parts, rather than two separate puffs of air.

Exercise 38

\	\	\	\	\	\	\	\	
ta	ta	ta	ta	ta	ta	ta	ta	
4	4	4	4	4	4	4	4	:||
e	e	e	e	e	e	e	e	

Using Partial Beats In The Train

Applying a more complex rhythm to the Train will make it more exciting and realistic sounding. Try tonguing a two syllable "Da ta", "Ta ta", or "Chuck-a" for each exhale chord of the train.

Whichever of these three doublet syllables you choose to use for your tonguing pattern, notice that the first syllable occurs when your foot hits the floor (directly under a timing slash), and the second syllable occurs in between taps (and between timing slashes).

Exercise 39

\	\	\	\	\	\
		ta	ta	ta	ta
456	456	456	456	456	456
i	i	e	e	e	e

\	\	\	\	\	\
		ta	ta	ta	ta
456	456	456	456	456	456
i	i	e	e	e	e

And if you've mastered your inhaled tonguing effect, tongue a "Da ta" or "Chukka" for each chord, exhale and inhale.

Exercise 40

\		\		\		\	
chuck	a	chuck	a	chuck	a	chuck	a
<u>456</u>	<u>456</u>	<u>456</u>	<u>456</u>	<u>456</u>	<u>456</u>	<u>456</u>	<u>456</u>
i	i	i	i	e	e	e	e

\		\		\		\	
chuck	a	chuck	a	chuck	a	chuck	a
<u>456</u>	<u>456</u>	<u>456</u>	<u>456</u>	<u>456</u>	<u>456</u>	<u>456</u>	<u>456</u>
i	i	i	i	e	e	e	e

Using Partial Beats In Songs

It is often possible to notate the timing of a song in more than one way. For example, in the previous notation for *Twinkle Twinkle Little Star*, each note was played for one beat. In the following notation version, many of the notes are only played for one half of a beat. Practice playing notes which do not occur on the beat, as indicated below.

Be sure to tap your foot only on the notes with timing slashes. You may find that the song has a "bouncier" or more "flowing" feeling to it, when played according to this notation. Otherwise it will sound exactly the same as the previous one note per beat version.

Twinkle Twinkle Little Star - 2

\	\	\	\	\	\	\	\
Twin	kle	twin	kle	lit	tle	star	
4	4	6	6	6	6	6	
e	e	e	e	i	i	e	
C				F		C	

\	\	\	\	\	\	\	\
How	I	won	der	what	you	are	
5	5	5	5	4	4	4	
i	i	e	e	i	i	e	
F		C		G		C	

\	\	\	\	\	\	\	\
Up	a	bove	the	world	so	high	
6	6	5	5	5	5	4	
e	e	i	i	e	e	i	
C		F		C		G	

\	\	\	\	\	\	\	\
Like	a	dia	mond	in	the	sky	
6	6	5	5	5	5	4	
e	e	i	i	e	e	i	
C		F		C		G	

\	\	\	\	\	\	\	\
Twin	kle	twin	kle	lit	tle	star	
4	4	6	6	6	6	6	
e	e	e	e	i	i	e	
C				F		C	

\	\	\	\	\	\	\	\
How	I	won	der	what	you	are	
5	5	5	5	4	4	4	
i	i	e	e	i	i	e	
F		C		G		C	

More Songs With Partial Beats

You may want to return to the one note per beat songs of Lesson Nine, and play them using partial beat rhythms rather than as notated previously. The following notation is probably considered more standard than the one note per beat versions, although both are perfectly acceptably. Additional folk, classical, and holiday songs that use partial beats are presented in Lessons Fifteen, Sixteen, Seventeen, and Eighteen. The last two of these songs feature three notes per beat, as described more fully in Lesson Fifteen. Here is the first line of each.

Exercise 41   *Good King Wenceslaus*

\	\	\	\	\	\	\	\	\	\	\	\
Good	king	Wen	ce	slas	look'd	out	On	the	feast	of	Ste	phen
7	7	7	8	7	7	6	6	6	6	7	7	7
e	e	e	i	e	e	e	i	e	i	i	e	e

Exercise 42   *Red River Valley*

\	\	\	\	\	\	\\
From	this	val	ley	they	say	you	are	go	ing
3	4	5	5	4	4	4	5	4	4
e	e	e	e	i	e	i	e	i	e

Exercise 43   *Amazing Grace*

\	\	\	\	\	\	\	\
A	maz	ing	grace	how	sweet	the	sound	to	save	a	wretch	like	me
6	7	8	8	8	7	6	6	6	7	8	8	8	9
e	e	e	e	i	e	i	e	e	e	e	e	i	e

Exercise 44   *For He's A Jolly Good Fellow*

\	\	\	\
For	he's	a	jol	ly	good	fel	low
4	5	5	5	4	5	5	5
e	e	e	e	i	e	i	e

Exercise 45   *On Top Of Old Smoky*

\	\	\	\	\	\\	\
On	top	of	old	Smo	ky		All	cov	ered	with	snow
4	4	5	6	7	6		6	5	6	6	6
e	e	e	e	e	i		i	i	e	i	e

Lesson 15
Rhythm Variations On The Doublet Pattern

The following rhythm patterns break certain beats into two parts. These rhythms, and variations built upon them, will be used to play blues and rock songs in later lessons. Although a number with a timing slash is meant to be played as one entire beat, it is acceptable to play it as a half or short note, and catch a quick breath during the rest of the beat, if desired. The ways in which these timing variations would be written in standard musical notation is explained in Appendix B at the end of this book.

A Blues Style Rhythm Pattern

This variation is simpler than the original doublet rhythm, since it leaves one entire beat in which to breathe. Do not omit the silent beat, represented by the slash without a note. It must be tapped out, mentally or by foot, before repeating the pattern.

Exercise 46

\	\	\	\
One	Two	and Three	(rest)

Exercise 47

\	\	\	\
ta	ta	ta ta	
4	4	4 4	
e	e	e e	

A Word To The Wise

Practice the Blues Style Rhythm Pattern above on the **123i** chord. If you eventually plan to work seriously in the blues genre, then practicing this pattern on the **2i** note by itself will also be useful. Re-read the end of Lesson Three if you find this difficult.

Exercise 48

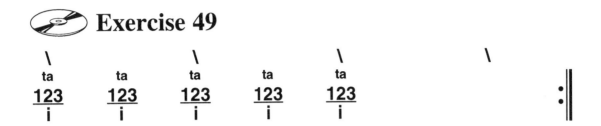

The Blues Style Rhythm Pattern may also be played with two notes on the first beat.

Exercise 49

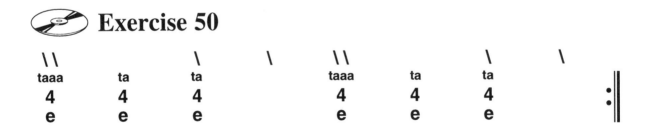

A Classical Style Rhythm Pattern

A portion of this pattern, in which a particular note is held for one-and-a-half beats, and the next note is held for one-half a beat, is common to many folk and classical songs. Practice to prepare for its use, with many variations, in the songs of the following lessons.

Exercise 50

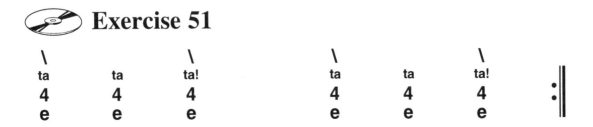

A Rock and Roll Style Rhythm Pattern

This pattern is a basic version of what is probably the most popular rock and roll rhythm. Try to emphasize the notes that fall on the second and fourth beats, as indicated by the explanation points on the tongueing.

Exercise 51

The Two-Timing Twelve Bar Blues

In the following verse, space has been conserved by placing the first repeat sign at the end of the top line, rather than writing the top two bars out twice. Thus the top line represents four, not two, bars.

Use a fast, fluttering hand vibrato on the long **45i** and long **45e** in the tenth and eleventh bars, and repeat the entire verse as indicated by the second repeat sign, at the end of the verse.

The No Frills Rollin' Rock

The following rock and roll style verse is based both on the Twelve Bar Chord Structure, and on the rock rhythm presented earlier in this lesson. Many rock songs, like this one, drop the chord change from D to C in the ninth and tenth bar by holding one chord (D) throughout both bars. This verse also omits the turnaround. On the recording, the first verse is played with more chords, and the second verse is played with more single notes.

As indicated by the exclamation point in the rock rhythm pattern described on page 54, rock songs usually place emphasis on the second and fourth beat of each bar. Also, notice that the first line must be repeated, as indicated by the repeat sign at its end.

```
| \   \ \   \   | \   \ \   \ :||
| 2 2 5 2 2 5 | 2 2 5 6        |
| i i i i i i | i i i e        |
  G

| \   \ \   \   | \   \ \   \   |
| 4 4 7 4 4 7 | 4 4 7 6        |
| e e e e e e | e e e e        |
  C

| \   \ \   \   | \   \ \   \   |
| 2 2 5 2 2 5 | 2 2 5 6        |
| i i i i i i | i i i e        |
  G

| \   \ \   \   | \   \ \   \   |
| 1 1 4 1 1 4 | 1 1 4 5        |
| i i i i i i | i i i i        |
  D

| \   \ \   \   | \   \ \   \ :||
| 2 2 5 2 2 5 | 2 2 5 6        |
| i i i i i i | i i i e        |
  G
```

Once again, if you have enjoyed these simple blues (and rock) pieces, you will find many more in *Progressive Blues Harmonica*, and *Progressive Blues Harmonica Licks Volumes One and Two*.

Lesson 16
More Songs That Use Partial Beats

These songs are no harder than the previous songs, except for the fact that they utilize partial beats as well as whole ones.

🎵 Taps

\	\\	\	\	\\	\	\	\	\	\	\	\
3	3	4	3	4	5	3	4	5	3	4	5
e	e	e	e	e	e	e	e	e	e	e	e
C											

\	\\	\	\	\\	\	\	\\	\	\	\	\\\\\\ \
3	4	5	4	5	6	5	4	3	3	3	4
e	e	e	e	e	e	e	e	e	e	e	e
								G			C

🎵 Old Folks At Home

\\	\		\	\	\	\	\	\\	\	\	\\\	\
Way	down	u	pon	the	Swan	ee	Riv	er		Far	far	a	way
5	4	4	5	4	4	7	6	7		6	5	4	4
e	i	e	e	i	e	e	i	e		e	e	e	i
C	F				C		F			C			G

\\	\		\	\	\	\	\		\
That's where	my	heart	is	turn	'in	e	ver	
5	4	4	5	4	4	7	6	7
e	i	e	e	i	e	e	i	e
C	F				C		F	

\	\	\	\	\\\	\	\\	\	\	\	\\	\	\
That's where	the	old	folks	stay		All	the	world	is	sad	and	drear	y
6	5	4	4	4	4	7	7	8	6	6	6	6	7
e	e	e	i	i	e	i	e	i	e	e	i	e	e
C			G		C	G				C			

\	\	\	\	\\\	\	\\	\	\	\	\	\	\	\
Ev	ry	where	I	roam		Oh	Lor	dy	how	my	heart	grows	wear	y
7	6	5	6	6		5	4	4	5	4	4	7	6	7
e	i	i	i	e		e	i	e	i	e	e	e	i	e
F				C		F			C			F		

\	\	\	\	\\\	\
Far	from	the	old	folks	at	home
6	5	4	4	4	4	4
e	e	e	i	i	e	
C			G		C	

My Country 'Tis Of Thee

\	\	\	\\	\	\	\
My	coun	try	tis	of	thee	sweet land
4	4	4	3	4	4	5 5
e	e	i	i	e	i	e e
C		Dm		G		C

\	\\	\	\	\	\	\\\	\
of	li	ber	ty	of	thee	I sing	
5	5	4	4	4	4	3 4	
i	e	i	e	i	e	i e	
				Dm	C	G C	

\	\	\	\\		\	\	\	\	\\		\
Land	where	my	fa	thers	died	land	of	the	pil	grims	pride
6	6	6	6	5	5	5	5	5	5	5	4
e	e	e	e	i	e	i	i	i	e	i	
					G						

\	\	\	\\		\	\	\	\	\\	\
From	ev	er	y	y	moun	tain	side	le	t	free dom ring
5	5	5	4	4	5	5	6	6	5	5 4 4
e	i	e	i	e	e	i	e	i	e	e i e
C								Dm		C G C

God Save The Queen

God save our gracious queen
Long live our noble queen
God save the queen
Send her victorious
Happy and glorious
Long to reign over us
God save the queen.

Lesson 17
About Classical Music

If you enjoy playing these pieces, you may wish to read Appendix B, on playing music from standard notation, and then obtain a book of simple classical pieces written for any instrument in the key of C. The following song is usually played using chords rather than single notes.

🎵 Ode to Joy (Beethoven's Ninth)

\	\	\	\	\	\	\	\	\	\	\	\	\\		\\
5	5	5	6	6	5	5	4	4	4	4	5	5	4	4
e	e	i	e	e	i	e	i	e	e	i	e	e	i	i
C													G7	

\	\	\	\	\	\	\	\	\	\	\	\	\\		\\
5	5	5	6	6	5	5	4	4	4	4	5	4	4	4
e	e	i	e	e	i	e	i	e	e	i	e	i	e	e
C												G	C	

\\	\	\	\	\		\	\	\	\		\	\	\	\	\\
4	5	4	4	5	5	5	4	4	5	5	5	4	4	4	3
i	e	e	i	e	i	e	e	i	e	i	e	i	e	i	e
G	C		G		C		G			C		Am	D	G	

\\	\	\	\	\	\	\	\	\	\	\	\\		\\
5	5	6	6	5	5	4	4	4	4	5	4	4	4
e	i	e	e	i	e	i	e	e	i	e	i	e	e
C					Am		Dm	C	G		C		

59

Brahm's Lullaby

```
\    \\   \    \\   \    \    \    \    \    \    \    \
5    5    6    5    5    6    5    6    7    7    6    6    6
e    e    e    e    e    e    e    e    e    i    i    i    e
C                                                  G

\    \    \    \    \    \\   \    \    \    \    \    \\
4    5    5    4    4    5    5    4    5    7    6    6    7    7
i    e    i    i    i    e    i    i    i    i    e    i    e
                                                            C

\    \\   \    \\   \    \    \    \    \    \
4    4    7    6    5    6    5    4    5    6    6    5    6
e    e    e    i    i    e    e    e    i    e    i    e    e
          F              C              F              C

\    \\   \    \\   \    \    \    \    \    \\
4    4    7    6    5    6    5    4    5    5    4    4
e    e    e    i    i    e    e    e    i    e    i    e
          F              C              G              C
```

Bach's Minuet In G (C, for You)

```
\    \    \    \    \    \    \    \    \    \    \    \    \    \
6    4    4    5    5    6    4    4    6    5    6    6    7    7    4    4
e    e    i    e    i    e    e    e    i    i    e    i    i    e    e    e
C                             F                        C

\    \    \    \    \    \    \    \    \    \    \    \\\
5    6    5    5    4    5    5    5    4    4    3    4    4    5    4    4
i    e    i    e    i    e    i    e    i    e    i    e    i    e    e    i
D                        C                   G

\    \    \    \    \    \    \    \    \    \    \    \    \    \
6    4    4    5    5    6    4    4    6    5    6    6    7    7    4    4
e    e    i    e    i    e    e    e    i    i    e    i    i    e    e    e
C                             F                        C

\    \    \    \    \    \    \    \    \    \    \    \\\
5    6    5    5    4    5    5    5    4    4    4    5    4    4    3    4
i    e    i    e    i    e    i    e    i    e    i    e    i    e    i    e
D                        C                   G                             C
```

Lesson 18
Some Holiday Hits

💿 *Silent Night*

\\	\	\\\	\\	\	\\\
Si	i	lent night	ho	o	ly night
6 6	6	5	6 6	6	5
e	i	e e	e	i	e e
C					

\\	\	\\\	\\	\	\\\
all	is	calm	all	is	bright
4 4	3	4	4 4	3	
i	i	i	e	e	e
G			**C**		

\\	\	\\	\	\\	\	\\\
Round yon	vi	i	gin	mo	ther and	child
6 6	7	7	6	6 6	6	5
i i	e	i	i	e	i e	e
F				**C**		

\\	\	\\	\	\\	\	\\\
ho	ly	in fant	so	ten der	and	mild
6 6	7	7	6	6 6	6	5
i i	e	i	i	e	i e	e
F				**C**		

\\	\	\\	\	\\\	\\\
Sleep	in	hea ven	ly	pea	ce
4 4	5	4	3	4	5
i i	i	i	i	e	e
G7				**C**	

\	\	\	\\	\	\\\\	\\
sle	ep	in	heav	en	ly	peace
7	6	5	6	5	4	4
e	e	e	e	i	i	e
G					**C**	

Auld Lang Syne

\	\\	\	\	\\		\	\	\\		\	\	\\\

Should auld   ac quaint ance   be   for   got and   ne   ver brought to mind?

3   4   3   4   5   4   4   4   5   4   4   5   6   6
e   e   i   e   e   i   e   i   e   e   e   e   e   i
C   **G**   **C**   **F**

Should auld   ac quaint ance   be   for   got and days   of   auld lang syne?

6   6   5   5   4   4   4   4   5   4   6   6   6   7
i   e   e   e   e   i   e   i   e   e   i   i   e   e
C   **G**   **F**   **C**

And days   of   auld   lang syne, my   dear, and days   of   auld lang syne,

6   6   5   5   4   4   4   4   6   6   5   5   6   6
i   e   e   e   e   i   e   i   i   e   e   e   e   i
                     G   **C**   **F**

Should auld   ac quaint ance   be   for   got and days   of   auld lang syne?

6   6   5   5   4   4   4   4   5   4   6   6   6   7
i   e   e   e   e   i   e   i   e   e   i   i   e   e
C   **G**   **F**   **C**

Jingle Bells

\	\	\	\		\	\			\\
Jin	gle	bells	jin	gle	bells	jin	gle	all	the	way
5	5	5	5	5	5	5	6	4	4	5
e	e	e	e	e	e	e	e	e	i	e
C										

\		\		\		\			\	\		\	\
oh	what	fun	it	is	to	ride	in	a	one	horse	o	pen	sle	igh
5	5	5	5	5	5	5	5	5	5	4	4	5	4	6
i	i	i	i	i	e	e	e	e	e	i	i	e	i	e
F					C				G					

\		\	\		\	\			\\
Jin	gle	bells	jin	gle	bells	jin	gle	all	the	way
5	5	5	5	5	5	5	6	4	4	5
e	e	e	e	e	e	e	e	e	i	e
C										

\		\		\		\			\		\	\\
Oh	what	fun	it	is	to	ride	in	a	one	horse	o	pen	sleigh
5	5	5	5	5	5	5	5	5	6	6	6	7	7
i	i	i	i	i	e	e	e	e	e	e	i	i	e
		F				C			G		F		C

Supplementary Songbook: Part Three

You may now begin to play the songs in the *Progressive Harmonica Supplementary Songbook*, Part Three.

Lesson 19
More Train Time

A more interesting train rendition can be performed with the addition of a whistle, to break up the chord sounds that mimic the noise of the wheels.

The Train Whistle

The hand vibrato can provide a fine whistle to go along with the train rhythm. Place your mouth over the single hole number 1, and inhale. Open and close your hands once per beat, with a beat of silence on the fourth beat. Repeat once for a two bar, or eight beat, train whistle.

💿 Exercise 52

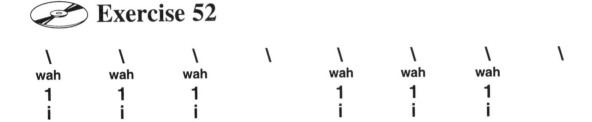

When you can play the above whistle, experiment with using three beats of fluttered hand vibrato for each bar of the whistle, then one silent beat.

💿 Exercise 53

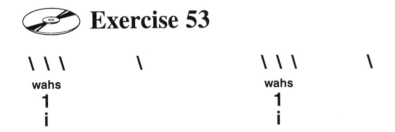

Or you may like to use the doublet style rhythm from Lesson Seven, with two double "wahs" and one single "wah" for each beat of whistle, as follows.

💿 Exercise 54

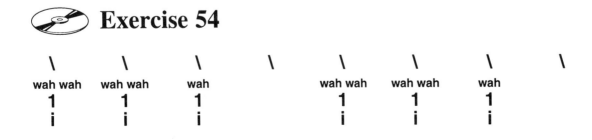

The Train With Whistle

The only hard thing about playing the Train With Whistle is going directly and with no break from the **456e** chord to the single note **1e**. Perhaps it is a bit like jumping onto a moving train — it takes determination, and a commitment without a great deal of thought.

It is easy to return to the **456i** chord from the second bar of **1e** whistle because you have a silent beat during which to breathe and locate the next chord. Begin slowly and carefully, without tonguing. Add the tonguing to the rhythm after you have mastered the move from the train to the whistle, and from the whistle to the train. Repeat the train for as long as you like before going to the whistle.

🎵 Exercise 55

\	\	\	\	\	\	\	\
456	456	456	456	456	456	456	456
i	i	e	e	i	i	e	e

\	\	\		\	\	\	\
wah	wah	wah		wah	wah	wah	
1	1	1		1	1	1	
i	i	i		i	i	i	

\	\	\	\	\	\	\	\
456	456	456	456	456	456	456	456
i	i	e	e	i	i	e	e

If you like, use a higher whistle for the train.

🎵 Exercise 56

\	\	\	\	\	\	\	\
456	456	456	456	456	456	456	456
i	i	e	e	i	i	e	e

\	\	\		\	\	\	\
wah	wah	wah		wah	wah	wah	
45	45	45		45	45	45	
i	i	i		i	i	i	

\	\	\	\	\	\	\	\
456	456	456	456	456	456	456	456
i	i	e	e	i	i	e	e

Experiment with this train. Play the train for a longer or shorter time before going to the whistle, or play the whistle for twice as long before returning to the train. Use tonguing on all or some of the beats, or don't, as you prefer. Vary the speed, and the loudness, and create your own interpretation of this classic harmonica piece.

💿 *Mister Lee's Freight Train*

This train uses some additional chords, and also varies the rhythm patterns. It is meant to be an example of a train, not one to be adhered to slavishly. It starts without any tonguing, then adds more complex tonguing rhythms. You may wish to practice each line separately before combining them. Play each line for as long as you wish, before going on to the next line. Note the use of the high chord **56i** for a whistle. Raising the pitch of the whistle adds a sense of urgency, as though the train is approaching the listener. Use the whistle in between the lines, or whenever it seems appropriate.

```
  \    \    \    \    \    \    \    \
 123  234  234  234  123  234  234  234   :||
  i    e    i    e    i    e    i    e

  \    \    \    \    \    \    \    \    \
 123  123  234  234  234  123  123  234  234  234   :||
  i    i    e    i    e    i    i    e    i    e

  \    \    \    \    \    \    \    \    \    \    \
 123  123  234  234  234  234  123  123  234  234  234  234   :||
  i    i    e    i    i    e    i    i    e    i    i    e

  \    \    \    \    \    \
 123  123  234  234  234  234  234  234   :||
  i    i    e    e    i    i    e    e

 \\\   \        \\\   \
  45             56              (whistle: insert as desired)
  i              i
```

Combine the lines, to form mixed rhythmic lines such as the following.

💿 Exercise 57

```
  \    \    \    \    \    \    \    \    \    \    \    \
 123  123  234  234  234  234  234  234  123  234  234  234   :||
  i    i    e    e    i    i    e    e    i    e    i    e
```

Lesson 20
Triplet Rhythms

This next song uses some beats that are broken into three parts instead of two, for the "mer-ri-ly's". This can be refered to as "triplet" timing. Practice triplet timing by saying "One and a Two and a Three and a Four" while tapping once for each number.

 Exercise 58

```
  \           \             \              \
one  and  a  two  and  a  three  and  a  four  :||
```

 Row Row Row Your Boat

\	\	\	\		\		\		\	\
Row	row	row	your	boat	gent	ly	down	the	stream	
4	4	4	4	5	5	4	5	5	6	
e	e	e	i	e	e	i	e	i	e	
C									G	

\			\			\			\		
Mer	ri	ly	mer	ri	ly	mer	ri	ly	mer	ri	ly
7	7	7	6	6	6	5	5	5	4	4	4
e	e	e	e	e	e	e	e	e	e	e	e
C											

\		\		\	\
life	is	but	a	dream	
6	5	5	4	4	
e	i	e	i	e	
G				C	

Fiddle Style or Bluegrass Harmonica

The American genre known as fiddle songs or Bluegrass features tunes that are usually of British-American extraction. They tend to be fast, with lots of notes. The following is one of the best-known fiddle songs.

Arkansaw Traveller

```
 \     \     \        \  \              \  \  \     \           \        \
 7  8  8  7  6  6  6  6  6  7  7  8  8  8  8  8  8  8  7  6
 e  e  i  e  i  i  i  e  e  e  e  i  e  e  i  e  i  i  i
 C           F           C           F     G7

 \     \     \        \  \     \  \  \
 6  7  8  8  7  6  6  6  6  6  7
 e  e  e  i  e  i  i  i  e  e
             C           F           C

 \     \     \        \        \        \     \
 7  7  7  6  6  7  6  5  5  4  4  3  4
 e  i  e  e  i  e  e  i  e  e  i  i  e
             F           C     G7    C

 \     \     \        \        \        \     \
 6  5  5  6  5  5  4  5  5  4  4  5  4  3  2
 e  i  e  e  i  e  i  i  e  e  e  i  i  i
             F           C              G7

 \  \  \  \     \     \
 4  4  4  4  4  5  4  4  5  4
 e  e  e  i  i  e  i  e  e  i
 C        G7    C        G7

 \     \     \        \     \     \        \        \
 5  5  6  5  5  6  5  5  4  5  5  4  4  5  4  3  2
 e  i  e  i  e  e  i  e  i  i  e  i  e  e  i  i  i
       C           F           C           G7

 \     \     \        \        \        \     \
 7  7  7  6  6  7  6  5  5  4  4  3  4
 e  i  e  e  i  e  e  i  e  e  i  i  e
 C           F           C     G7    C
```

💿 Irish Washerwoman

You can begin to practice this famous jig by playing it with one beat per note, but it will sound best when played with a triplet beat.

```
        \       \       \       \
6 5 5 4 4 3 4 4 5 4 5 6 5 5
e i e e e e e e e e e i e
C

\       \       \       \
5 4 4 2 4 4 5 4 5 6 6 5
i i i i i i i i i e i
G7

\       \       \       \       \       \       \       \
5 4 4 3 4 4 5 4 5 6 5 5 5 4 4 4 6 5 5 4 4 4
e e e e e e e e e i e i i i e i e e e
C                               G7              C

        \       \       \       \       \       \       \
4 4 5 4 5 4 5 4 5 4 4 4 3 4 3 4 3 4 4 4
e i e e e e e e e i e i i i i i i e i
                                G7

\       \       \       \       \       \       \
5 4 5 4 5 4 3 2   5 5 4 4 6 5 5 4 4 4
e e e e e e e e   i e i i e i e e e
C                 G7              C
```

🎵4 *Supplementary Songbook: Part Four*

You are now ready to begin playing the songs in Part Four of the *Progressive Harmonica Supplementary Songbook*.

Lesson 21
Playing The Minor Scale

After the Major Scale, the second most popular scale is the Minor Scale. It can be most easily played between holes 6 and 10, although all of the notes, with one exception, are also available between holes 3 and 6.

Exercise 59

The High Minor Scale:	A	B	C	D	E	F	G	A
	6	7	7	8	8	9	9	10
	i	i	e	i	e	i	e	i

Playing The Reverse High Minor Scale

You'll be able to play the following songs easily if you practice playing the Minor Scale from high end to low end also.

Exercise 60

Reverse Minor Scale:	10	9	9	8	8	7	7	6
	i	e	i	e	i	e	i	i

The Lower Minor Scale

It will be easier to begin working on the lower Minor Scale in reverse, since the missing note is the first note of the scale. Here are the notes of the low Minor Scale (reversed) with the missing A note indicated.

A	G	F	E	D	C	B	(A)
6	6	5	5	4	4	3	X
i	e	i	e	i	e	i	X

Now try two alternative ways of playing it by using octave substitution, both reverse and regular. As explained in *Progressive Blues Harmonica*, the missing A note can also be played using the advanced blues harmonica technique of "bending" (not shown).

Exercise 61

A	G	F	E	D	C	B	A
6	6	5	5	4	4	3	6
i	e	i	e	i	e	i	i

Exercise 62

A	G	F	E	D	C	B	A
6	7	4	4	5	5	6	6
i	i	e	i	e	i	e	i

Greensleeves

A few notes have been changed to make this romantic song easier to play without bending. It is normally notated with half as many timing slashes, but may be easier to read and play as follows.

```
\     \\    \     \     \     \     \\    \     \     \
A     las   my    lo    ve    you   do    me    wro   ng
6     7     8     8     9     8     8     7     6     6
i     e     i     e     i     e     i     i     e     i
Am                            G

\     \\    \     \     \     \     \\    \     \\    \
to    cast  me    of    ff    dis   court eous  ly
7     7     6     6     6     6     7     6     5
i     e     i     i     e     i     i     e     e
Am                                  E

\     \\    \     \     \     \     \\    \     \     \
And   I     have  lov   e     ed    you   so    lo    ng
6     7     8     8     9     8     8     7     6     6
i     e     i     e     i     e     i     i     e     i
Am                                  G

\     \     \     \     \     \     \     \\    \     \     \\
de    li    ght   ing   i     n     your  com   pa    ny
7     7     7     6     6     5     6     6     6     6
i     e     i     i     e     e     e     i     i     i
Am                      E7                Am

\\\   \     \     \     \\    \     \     \     \
Green sle   eves  was   all   my    j     o     y
9     9     9     8     8     7     6     6     7
e     e     i     e     i     i     e     i     i
C                             G

\\    \     \     \     \     \\    \     \\\
Gre   en    slee  ves   was   my    de    light
7     6     6     6     6     7     6     5
e     i     i     e     i     i     e     e
Am                                  E

\\\   \     \     \     \\    \     \     \
Green slee  ves   my    heart of    go    ld
9     9     9     8     8     7     6     6
e     e     i     e     i     i     e     i
C                             G

\     \     \     \     \     \     \     \\\   \\
And   who   but   my    la    -     dy    Green sleeves
7     7     7     6     6     5     6     6     6
i     e     i     i     e     e     e     i     i
        Am                  E                 Am
```

God Rest Ye Merry Gentlemen

	\	\	\	\	\	\	\	\	\	\	\	\	\\	\
	God	rest	ye	mer	ry	gen	tle	men	let	noth	ing	ye	dis	may
	6	6	8	8	8	7	7	6	6	6	7	7	8	8
	i	i	e	e	i	e	i	i	e	i	i	e	i	e
	Am		E7		Am					F				E7

\	\	\	\	\	\	\	\	\	\	\	\	\\	\
re	mem	ber	Christ	our	sav	i	or	was	born	on	Christ	mas	day
6	6	8	8	8	7	7	6	6	6	7	7	8	8
i	i	e	e	i	e	i	i	e	i	i	e	i	e
Am		E7		Am					F				E7

\	\	\	\	\	\	\	\	\	\	\	\	\\
To	save	us	all	from	Sa	tan's	power	if	we	were	gone	a	stray
8	9	8	8	9	9	10	8	8	7	6	7	7	8
e	i	i	e	i	e	i	e	i	e	i	i	e	i
F				C				Am				G7

\	\	\\	\	\	\	\	\	\	\		\	\	\	\
O	oh	ti	dings	of	co	om	fort	and	joy		com	fort	and	joy
7	8	8	9	8	8	8	7	7	6		7	7	6	8
e	i	e	i	e	e	i	e	i			e	i	i	i
		Am			E7				Am					G7

\	\	\	\	\	\	\	\	\	\	\\\	\\\\
O	oh	ti	i	dings	of	co	om	fort	and	joy	
7	8	8	9	9	10	8	8	7	7	6	
e	i	e	i	e	i	e	i	e	i	i	
		Am			E7				Am		

Many more songs, most characterized by a mournful or wistful quality, can be played using the Minor Scale. Some of these include *When Johnny Comes Marchin' Home Again*, *Hatikvah*, the *Chanukah Song*, *Summertime*, and *Autumn Leaves*.

Supplementary Songbook: Part Five

You are now ready to begin playing the songs in Part Five of the *Progressive Harmonica Supplementary Songbook*.

Lesson 22
Playing The Dorian Scale

There are two more Scales, after the Major Scale and Minor Scale, that every serious harmonica player must learn. The first of these is the Dorian Scale, sometimes called the Dorian Minor Scale. It can be used to play songs in musical traditions as diverse as those of the blues and sea chanteys.

The Dorian Scale, which when used in the blues tradition forms the basis for Third Position blues harmonica playing, as explained in *Progressive Blues Harmonica*, is most easily played between the 4 and 8 holes without need for bending.

Exercise 63

The Dorian Scale:	A	B	C	D	E	F	G	A
	4	5	5	6	6	7	7	8
	i	e	i	e	i	i	e	i

Playing The Reverse Dorian Scale

You'll be able to play the following songs easily if you practice playing the Dorian Scale from high end to low end also.

Exercise 64

Reverse Dorian Scale:	8	7	7	6	6	5	5	4
	i	e	i	i	e	i	e	i

Saint James Infirmary

```
  \         \    \         \    \          \        \\\
  Well  I   went down to   St.  James In   firm ry
  4     5   6    6    5    6    6     6    5    4
  i     i   i    i    i    6    6     6    5    4
                             e    i     e    i    i
  Dm                  Gm              Dm

  \         \    \         \    \    \     \\\
  My    ba  by   was  a    lay  in   there
  4     6   6    6    6    8    8    6
  i     i   i    i    i    e    i    i
                        Gm        Dm

  \         \    \         \    \         \    \\\
  Stretched out  on   a    long wh   ite  ta   ble
  6     6   6    5    6    6    6    5    4
  i     i   i    i    i    e    i    i
                        Gm        Dm

        \         \         \    \    \    \    \\
  so    young I   said Oh   Lord it   ain't fair
  4     5   4    5    6    6    6    5    4
  i     i   i    i    e    i    e    i    i
  B♭              A7             Dm
```

House of the Rising Sun

```
  \    \    \    \    \    \    \    \    \    \    \
  There is  a    house in  New  Or   leans they call the  Ris  ing  Sun
  6    8    8    7    6    6    4    5    6    6    7    6    6    6
  i    i    i    e    i    e    i    i    e    i    e    i    e    i
  Dm             F         G         B♭        Dm             F         A7

        \         \         \         \
  And   its been  the  ruin of   ma   ny   poor boys
  6     7   8     8    7    6    6    5    4    5
  i     e   i     i    e    i    e    i    i    i
        Dm        F         G              B♭

        \         \              \    \
  Ah    me   I    kn   ow   I'm  one  oh!
  5     4    5    5    5    5    4    6
  i     i    i    e    i    e    i    i
  Dm              A7             Dm
```

What Shall We Do With A Drunken Sailor

\			\			\		\	
What	shall	we	do	with	a	drunk	en	sail	or
6	6	6	6	6	6	6	4	5	6
i	i	i	i	i	i	i	i	i	i
Dm									

\			\			\		\	
What	shall	we	do	with	a	drunk	en	sail	or
6	6	6	6	6	6	6	4	5	6
e	e	e	e	e	e	e	e	e	e
C									

\			\			\		\	
What	shall	we	do	with	a	drunk	en	sail	or
6	6	6	6	6	6	6	7	7	8
i	i	i	i	i	i	i	i	e	i
Dm									

\		\		\	\
Ear	ly	in	the	mor	ning
7	6	6	5	4	4
e	i	e	e	i	i
C				Dm	

 ## Supplementary Songbook: Part Six

You are now ready to begin playing the songs in Part Six of the *Progressive Harmonica Supplementary Songbook*.

Appendix A:
Playing With Others

Playing Along With Recordings

Playing along with recordings is an excellent way of honing your harmonica skills. It is important to make certain that you are playing along in the correct key, however. Your C harmonica can be easily played in four different keys: C Major, A Minor, D Dorian, and G Blues, reflecting the scales studied in this book.

As you already know, folk songs will probably be Major, unless they have the plaintive quality that often accompanies the Minor Scale. Blues songs will tend to use the Blues Scale. Play each likely scale along with a song that you like, and if one sounds right, you are probably in the correct key. Unfortunately, without having a harmonica in all twelve different keys, there will be many songs that you cannot accompany.

Which Key Harmonica To Buy Next

When choosing additional harmonicas, you will find the following most useful and versatile, in this order: A, G, D, and E for playing with guitars, F and G for playing with keyboards, and B♭, F, and E♭ for playing with horns. Although they may be enjoyable for solo playing, D♯ (or E♭), B, F♯ (or G♭), C♯ (or D♭), and G♯ (or A♭) are usually not too useful for playing with recordings or other musicians.

Playing With Other Musicians

When playing with other musicians, always ask what key the song to be played will be in, and, if possible, whether it uses mostly Major, Minor, Dorian, or Blues scales or chords. At first, try to stick to the songs in this book, since you already know what scales to use with them.

Major songs will be most easily played if the key of your harmonica is the same as the key of the song, that is, in First Position. With your C harmonica, this will mean playing songs in C.

Blues songs will be most easily played if the key of your harmonica is five half steps up from the key of the song, that is, in Second or Cross Position. One half step is the distance between any two notes on the piano that are next to each other. With your C harmonica, this will mean playing blues in G.

Minor songs will be most easily played if the key of your harmonica is three half steps down from the key of the song. With your C harmonica, this will mean playing Minor songs in A.

Dorian songs will be most easily played if the key of your harmonica is two half steps up from the key of the song. With your C harmonica, this will mean playing Dorian songs in D.

The following chart will help you decide which harmonica to use when playing with other musicians. Decide what key the song is in, then locate that key in the top row, above the columns of the chart. Then decide whether it is Major, Minor, Dorian, or Blues, and locate the correct row along the side of the chart. Where the row and column intersect, you will find the correct key harmonica to use. For example, if you know that a song is in the key of A, and it is a Minor song, you will want to use a C harmonica (look down the A column until you reach the third, or Minor, row). For your convenience, all of the places in which a C harmonica can be used have been indicated in outline type: Major in C, Minor in A. Dorian in D, and Blues in G.

KEY OF SONG:	C	C♯	D	D♯	E	F	F♯	G	G♯	A	A♯	B
h MAJOR:	Ⓒ	C♯	D	D♯	E	F	F♯	G	G♯	A	A♯	B
a MINOR:	D♯	E	F	F♯	G	G♯	A	A♯	B	Ⓒ	C♯	D
r DORIAN:	A♯	B	Ⓒ	C♯	D	D♯	E	F	F♯	G	G♯	A
p BLUES:	F	F♯	G	G♯	A	A♯	B	Ⓒ	C♯	D	D♯	E

This chart can also be used to help you and your musical partners decide what key song to play. For instance, if they wish to play a song in a Minor key, and you have only a C harmonica, you will look in the Minor Row (third from top) until you see a C, then look to the top of that column to find out what Minor key song will work with a C harmonica (an A Minor song). If you have A, C and G harmonicas and want to play blues with other musicians, look for the A, C and G in the Blues (bottom) row, then look to the top row to find that you can play Blues in E, G, and D.

Timing And Other Musicians

Tap your feet together to make sure that you agree on the timing of the song, and remember that the rhythm notation of songs in this book may sometimes double the number of taps per note, for ease of reading. If you are tapping together but your song seems to be much slower than theirs, this may be the case. Also, as explained in great detail in *Progressive Blues Harmonica*, many Blues and Jazz songs "swing" the beat, a subtle but important rhythmic variation that is beyond the scope of this book.

About The *Supplementary Songbook*

If you would like to have additional songs to play while you are using the *Progressive Harmonica Method*, you may wish to obtain the *Progressive Harmonica Supplementary Songbook*. It contains six sets of songs, with Part One graded for use after you have completed Lesson 8 of the *Progressive Harmonica Method*, Part Two for use after Lesson 11, Part Three after Lesson 18, Part Four after Lesson 20, Part Five after Lesson 21, and Part Six after Lesson 22. Many more favourite songs are included in the *Progressive Harmonica Supplementary Songbook* and a recording is available as well.

About *Progressive Blues Harmonica*

The first few Lessons of *Progressive Blues Harmonica* are similar to the first lessons of *Progressive Harmonica Method*, so as to enable readers to use each book independently. Later lessons cover blues material in greater detail, including "first position", "second" or "cross position", and "third position" playing. Many examples of blues, boogie woogie, and rock songs and riffs are provided, as well as instructions on bending techniques, creative improvisation, swinging the beat, tonal effects, some blues style folk songs, and how to play a blues train. A recording is available to accompany the *Progressive Blues Harmonica* book, as are two additional books, *Progressive Blues Harmonica Licks Volume One and Two* and their recordings.

Appendix B:
Reading Standard Notation For The Harmonica

Although standard musical notation is a wonderfully useful musical language that allows musicians to communicate accurately with each other, it is not a language well-suited for the ten hole harmonica. Harmonicas come in each of the twelve different keys, and harmonica players must change the key that they use to play songs in different keys. Thus reading standard notation involves learning twelve different systems for a harmonica player, one for each key, unlike most other instrumentalists, who must learn only one system.

However, for those of you who can already read standard notation, following is sufficient information to allow you to read for harmonica in the key of C. If you like, you can play any song using C notation as described below for harmonica, but by using a harmonica in a different key, produce the song in that key. For example, playing the standard notation provided below for Twinkle Twinkle Little Star with a G harmonica will produce the song in G, playing the same notation with an E flat harmonica will produce the song in E flat.

Standard Notation and Harmonica Rhythm Notation

This is how the rhythm notation in this book compares to standard musical rhythm notation, written for the **4e** note. Notice that in the last example, below, the first 4e note of the two gets one and one-half beat, and the second 4e note of the two gets one-half beat, as indicated by the dotted quarter note and eighth note.

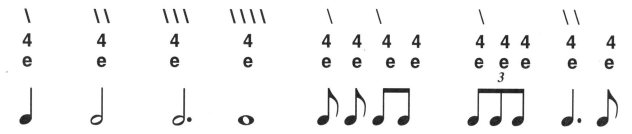

Standard Notation and The Notes of the C Harmonica

The three complete octaves of the C harmonica begin with the the note middle C on the treble clef. The highest octave 7e through 10e is written the same as the middle octave 4e through 7e, with the notation *8va* written above any high section to indicate that the section should be played one octave higher than written.

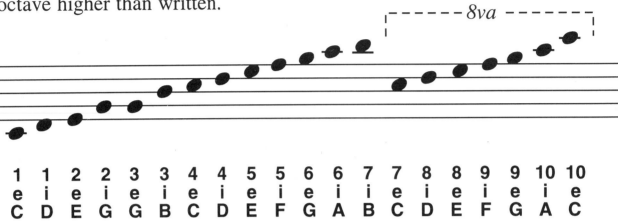

1	1	2	2	3	3	4	4	5	5	6	6	7	7	8	8	9	9	10	10
e	i	e	i	e	i	e	i	e	i	e	i	e	i	e	i	e	i	e	i
C	D	E	G	G	B	C	D	E	F	G	A	B	C	D	E	F	G	A	C

And here is a simple example of part of a song, written in both harmonica notation for a key of C harmonica, and in standard musical notation along with the letter names of the notes.

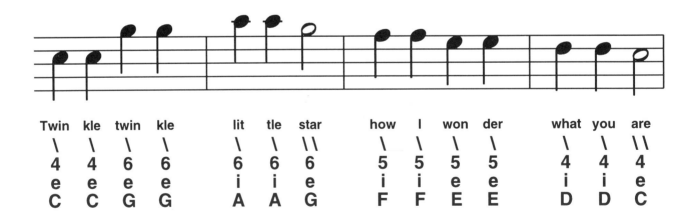

Twin	kle	twin	kle	lit	tle	star	how	I	won	der	what	you	are
\	\	\	\	\	\	\\	\	\	\	\	\	\	\\
4	4	6	6	6	6	6	5	5	5	5	4	4	4
e	e	e	e	i	i	e	i	i	e	e	i	i	e
C	C	G	G	A	A	G	F	F	E	E	D	D	C